SEX
IN THE EXECUTIVE
SUITE

SEX
IN THE EXECUTIVE
SUITE

H. Paul Jeffers and Dick Levitan

ᑫ❤P
A Playboy Press Book

Contents

CONTENTS

Introduction

When we undertook the writing of this book about sex in American business, we wondered if we were heading into the trap that humorist Robert Benchley warned about when he said, "The only thing that the sex psychologists can't read a sexual significance into is trap-shooting, and they are working on that now." With our research completed and the book written, we do not feel that we ventured into a topic that was more legend than fact. We have not read anything into what we learned.

Sex *is* an integral part of the way Americans do business. In many cases it is the *only* way they do business.

What really surprised us was the readiness of people to tell us all about it. The most casual mention of the book's subject was invariably met with an eager willingness to tell us all we wanted to know. "Have I got a story for your book!" Gratefully we listened and taped the tales that the people of the executive suites of America were so eager to relate. To be sure, this readiness to lift the veil was reinforced by our assurances that what we learned would be held in the strictest confidence. That is, we weren't going to name names. We haven't. Except where names of people appeared in the public records of the police or the courts, names in this book have been changed. Also, locations have been switched where they might have indirectly revealed identities of persons.

We have tried to cover the whole spectrum of American business and to determine what impact sex has on it. The effect is staggering, leading us to the conclusion that sex is as important to the way Americans do business as computers, the telephone, and the assembly line.

Of necessity, this book deals with prostitution. Firms ranging from the largest corporate conglomerates to the tiniest one-man businesses engage prostitutes, madams, and pimps to win contracts, entice customers, and keep the balance sheets tilted to the profit side. To the extent that we deal with prostitution, we do so only in terms of prostitution and prostitutes as tools of business. We try, also, to understand why some successful executives pursue sex with prostitutes for personal satisfaction as well as for business goals.

We directed much of this study of sex in the executive suite to the people themselves—their motives, their needs, their objectives—because we became convinced that anyone who has a white-collar job in American business is likely to be confronted with sex as an ingredient of their daily work.

Because of the nature of this book we cannot personally acknowledge the many people who were helpful to us. However, we can express our thanks to Trudy Levitan for transcribing hours of taped interviews and for giving us insights into the material and the people involved in those tapes which formed the basis for this study; her patience and understanding were and are invaluable.

H. Paul Jeffers and Dick Levitan
New York City

1
Secretary Wanted

The young woman clutched her negligee at the neck and held it closed against a chill wind that came up suddenly from a small park many floors below the terrace where she stood. The chill sent a shudder through her small, shapely body and raised goose bumps on her pale skin. The breeze shaped her negligee to her naked body beneath and caught her long, free, yellow hair and laced it across her face in tickling strands. She pushed her hair back, turned, and stepped from the terrace through wide French doors into a splendid hotel suite with gold wall coverings, period furniture, and deep, soft carpeting. On bare feet she crossed the room and stood by the bed. She looked down at a man asleep on the bed. He slept naked, breathing restfully. His features were relaxed. Earlier, he had been wildly passionate, moving strongly, demandingly, urgently. Now, he slept like a child, she thought, as she bent over the man and touched him on the shoulder.

He startled awake. "Did I fall asleep?" he muttered. The young woman nodded and smiled. "Sorry," he said, reaching to her and stroking her thigh through the negligee.

"We should be getting back. There's that meeting to prepare for," she said.

The man lifted his hand and pushed it beneath the filmy negligee, resting it upon her naked breast, squeezing gently. "You are the perfect secretary," he said as he pushed himself up from the bed and put his lips against hers.

"The perfect boss," she sighed, slipping back with him onto the bed.

The negligee parted and he stretched himself upon her, kissing her mouth, chin, ears, and neck as they began again the lovemaking that had been their afternoons for ten months.

Half an hour later she left the suite alone and returned to her job. Fifteen minutes after her return he walked into the office, strode past her desk, and entered his own office. He pulled off his jacket, sat at his desk, pressed the intercom button, and said, "Okay, Penny, let's tackle that stuff for the meeting."

For ten months this young executive and his secretary had been slipping away from their work to the hotel suite maintained by their company. He had chosen the hotel and the suite and authorized its use and the monthly rental. Such matters were part of his job's responsibilities. A similar suite at a hotel across town had been arranged by him for the president of the firm.

Neither this arrangement, the affair between the young man and his secretary, nor the financing of their rendez-vous from company resources seemed to them unusual in any way; in fact, they were not unusual. They were simply part of the whole fabric of sex in the executive suite: getting it, giving it, using it. On getting it, giving it, and using it turns the world of business because in that world one is either a getter, giver, or user. Prices vary, but there is always a price attached—a deal locked up, a promotion garnered, a job secured, money earned, ego fed, duty fulfilled, reward attained.

This, then, is the world awaiting the young woman who launches herself into a career in business.

Running her long, beautifully manicured finger down the want ads, K found what she was looking for: "SECRE-TARY-GAL FRIDAY to assume total responsibility in one-girl office for busy financier. Good steno and typing skills. Must be able to handle own correspondence. Person-able, young, good conversation. Reply stating salary to Box——."

Excitedly, K circled the ad, then perfunctorily scanned the others. She knew she had found what she was looking for and felt a surging confidence that she would be right for the job. She found encouragement in the fact that the written inquiry was expected. She wrote well and also knew that many girls would avoid applying for a job that required a letter rather than a phone call. She dashed off a very good letter on her portable machine, then hurried to the lobby of her apartment house to mail it.

K had come from a small town in New Jersey. She was sufficiently pretty, bright, and sophisticated to know that she would have to get out of that town to be successful, and success was what she hungered for. To be someone had always been the driving force in her life, whether it was being popular at school, winning school elections, or coming out on top in the world of business. Success was a specter over her family. Her father had never achieved it, and her mother never failed to remind him of that painful fact. K carried memories of conversations—argu-ments, really—in which her mother humiliated her father because he had not accomplished more.

Escaping her family and her home town at last, K found work in New York City as a stenographer, one of a dozen girls in the steno pool. But she was far from satisfied, and she believed that the advertisement that she had answered would open doors for her. She was not at all surprised when she was asked to appear for a personal interview.

She decided that a man in finance would appreciate the conservative, so she chose an outfit accordingly. On a cold and slushy January day, she went to the office for the interview wearing an expensively tailored brown skirt, coordinated blazer, and gold turtleneck dickey, with little make-up.

The office was as she expected. Even on a gray day it was cheery.

The man who interviewed her was in his midforties, balding, quite short. Balanced on his nose—of all things, K thought—rose-tinted glasses. He smiled and said, "Hello." His office was as handsome as the outer one, although larger and brighter. Windows provided a spectacular view of midtown. The man got down to business in an interview that was surprisingly chatty. He talked to K about her background and family more than about her secretarial ability. He complimented her on her vocabulary, her fine speech, and her good grooming. "But," he said, "I think for this position something a little less conservative would be in order. We'll have to see that you get a new wardrobe."

K smiled at the realization that this pleasant man had apparently decided to hire her, but she felt a certain vague uneasiness, a feeling that was to grow in the next few moments to near panic.

"My gal Friday," he said with a light touch, "will have to keep some unusual hours. Much of my business is done in a social setting. You know, over drinks and dinner, maybe over supper after the theater. Many of the gentlemen with whom I do business are from out of town, and they like the idea of being wined and dined while they talk business. And it never hurts to have an attractive and accommodating escort."

He paused. Behind the rose-tinted glasses his heavy eyebrows arched up slightly, adding a question mark to the statement he had just made. The brows had lifted as he spoke the word "accommodating," and K saw with clarity what her prospective employer was getting at.

"Do you think you would be interested in the position?" he asked.

K clutched her handbag and sat up straight. "It certainly sounds like an interesting job," she said politely, "but I'm not sure I would be able to give it all the time that you apparently expect."

"We haven't discussed salary, but I assure you the unusual hours would be reflected handsomely in the salary." He glanced at her letter lying on his desk. "It is well above what you indicate here you are now earning."

"It is a very attractive offer. . . ."

"Very attractive," he emphasized, "and a job that has a lot of glamour and excitement over and above the salary." He glanced across his desk, peering over the tops of the rose-tinted glasses. "I'll tell you what. You take a day or two and think about it. Give me a call either way. Okay?"

K nodded. "Okay."

Passing from the spacious office with its spectacular view, through the bright, comfortable, cheery office that could be hers, K stepped into the corridor as the man in the rose-tinted glasses closed the door behind her. She walked slowly toward the elevator. Waiting for it to come, she turned and looked back at the door with a realization that she was no longer shocked by what the man had presumably been suggesting to her. She was becoming fascinated by the idea and was interested to discover that she was, in her mind, actually weighing the possibilities opened, however obliquely, by the conversation. By the time the elevator had whisked her to the ground floor, K knew that she would not immediately dismiss this job from her consideration.

Two days later she picked up the telephone and dialed the number she had been given. When she heard the mellow baritone of the man in the rose-tinted glasses, she told him she would take the job.

The following Monday, in stylish evening clothes and a modest fur coat, she accompanied her boss and a client to dinner at The Four Seasons. When her boss left her and the client alone for after-dinner brandy, it never occurred to K to think of herself as a prostitute.

Sex in the executive suite is rarely regarded that way.

In a few short years K has risen in the world of business and now has an office of her own in the executive suite.

"I remember reading one of those magazine articles that gives advice to girls coming to New York to look for careers," K recalls, "and the article said something to the effect that moving up in the business world is rarely a case of working your way to the top. You do it in zigs and zags, job-hopping. That's how I did it."

She smiles a contented, self-satisfied smile, and it is not so much that she has made it in a man's world as the realization that she has made her success on her own terms that evokes the smile. She admits she had misgivings about the beginning, about that first job interview, about the first time she went to bed with a man as part of a commercial undertaking.

"After that first job, that initiation, I saw what the pattern was, and I used the pattern to my advantage. I worked with that first guy for about a year. Then I met one of his clients, a San Francisco importer. That was the second step up the ladder," K recalls. She smiles again, and the smile becomes a laugh. "We were in bed in one of the hotels, the Plaza, I think, and he was very turned on to me. I was doing all the little things that a woman can do to drive a man crazy. He was begging me to finish it off. I kind of snuggled up to him, put my chin right against his, and asked him to take me back to San Francisco with him.

" 'Anything you want, baby,' he sighed."

Quite serious again, K fixes her green eyes on some distant point. "That's the way it's been all along. Anything I want."

In a flurry of activity K began moving from New York City to San Francisco, a city she had never visited but had admired from a distance.

The job was not much. A low-level secretary. Just above the steno pool. It was barely enough money to pay for an apartment K found atop one of San Francisco's hills. "It's just for the sake of appearances now, baby," explained her new employer. "In a couple of months you'll be moving. There's an opening coming up that will suit you perfectly. Of course you'll have to talk it over with the man you'll be working for. He's just below me on the organization chart."

He was a very quiet person, just over forty, with a wife and kids tucked away in a pleasant house beyond the Golden Gate Bridge in Marin County. He seemed very straight, but K had long abandoned outward appearances as clues to character.

The job interview was in three stages: drinks at The Crown atop the Fairmont Hotel, affording a view of the whole Bay Area from a revolving cocktail lounge; dinner at Le Boeuf—steaks, of course; and a nightcap in a small apartment, out of the way, maintained by the import company for the convenience of its clients.

"Once a week my boss made an excuse to work late at the office. We would go to that cute little company apartment, and I remember how very sophisticated I felt making love to him with the sound of cable-car bells in the distance," K recalls.

Occasionally business required an out-of-town trip.

"There was one long weekend in Las Vegas that has to stack up well in comparison to any orgy that ever happened there," K notes. "Another trip to Los Angeles was quite the opposite. Just the two of us in the Sheraton Universal. We both thought Hollywood was tacky. Then there was a one-day quickie down the coast to Monterey. The boss drove. The day was magnificent. We were in a convertible. Just because I wanted to, as we were taking those Route One curves around those steep cliffs just over the ocean, I snuggled my head down into his lap and made him come with my mouth."

K pauses a long time, remembering.

"Then it was back to New York. Back to the Big Apple."

The move back to New York was under circumstances similar to those which took her West. "I met a man. He liked me. He had a job for me."

Executive secretary.

K paused outside her office and stared for a long time at the sign above her name. She entered the office with a confident stride and greeted *her* personal secretary with a warm "Hi."

Sitting behind her large teakwood desk in the spacious office adjoining the office of the president of one of the largest import-export corporations in the world, K turned philosophical, something she does often.

"That first day in that job in that really gorgeous office at one of New York's best addresses, I thought about the road I'd taken to get there. Everyone is reflective at a time like that. You notice the milestones along the way. Any regrets? None. It was the smart way."

Not everyone applying for a job as secretary remains as cool about it as K when it becomes apparent that the job might possibly include extracurricular sex. Witness a recent letter to "Dear Abby" (Abigail Van Buren):

DEAR ABBY: I have just returned from an interview for a secretarial position. The boss himself interviewed me, and I must say, I was surprised at some of the questions he asked me.

He wanted to know if I was on "the Pill." (I had already told him I was recently divorced.)

Then he asked, "Do you drink?" I told him I didn't. Then he smiled and added, "Not even a little social drinking once in a while?" I said, "No. I just don't care for it." Then he looked at me like I was some kind of oddball.

He also asked me if I ever "turned on" with drugs. By that time I had had it, and replied, "Good grief, no!"

I doubt if that interview will result in a job offer. But if it does, I shall turn it down.

Not having sought employment for 10 years, perhaps I am out of touch with today's scene. But I'd like to know if these questions are routine in an interview today? Or did this particular man have something else in mind?

SHOCKED IN
MANHATTAN

DEAR SHOCKED: The questions you were asked were not routine, and I suspect that man who interviewed you had fringe benefits in mind. For HIM— not you.

If we might be permitted a reply of our own:

Dear Abby: Don't kid yourself! What happened to "Shocked in Manhattan" happens quite a lot and is far more routine than you'd expect. There are certain signals that will let a job interviewer know if it is safe to press ahead into matters having nothing to do directly with the job in question. The green light in "Shocked's" interview was the mention of her divorce. Other green lights include the manner of dress, the way a girl walks and sits, and her general demeanor.

The sexual stalking that goes on in the executive suite *often* starts in the job interview!

For Ellen it was television that provided a way to the top. Studying mass communications at Boston University, Ellen picked up a part-time job as an assistant to a production manager at a TV station in New England. "I came into that operation at the peak of a very bitter internal political struggle," she recalls. "My boss was pitted against another station executive. At stake was the top job, general manager. I figured that my future was with the guy I was working for. If he didn't come out on top, he and all who worked for him would be out the door. Well, there was a very nice boy in the other camp, so to speak. He was very close to the other executive. So I made it my business to get close to that boy. He was a very sweet boy, very naïve. I honestly think he was a virgin. He used to take work home with him to his place, and when we'd go back there after a date and have sex, I just kind of floated around his pad, poking around. I learned a lot of things that I passed on to my boss. He got the top job, and I became his personal assistant. Later I came to New York. At the networks it's the same, but more intense. I play the game there too, and it's worked out. A lot of it is luck, but mostly it's a matter of knowing what side to take. I don't want you to feel that the way to get ahead is by sleeping around with everyone. You have to be selective about who you give it to. And it's never for free."

American business runs on profit, and all who take part

expect to share in the profit in some form or other—
dividends, wages, bonuses, incentives. If sex enhances the
profits, fine!

Tracy is a stunningly beautiful publicist for a national
magazine. She remembers the Greenwich Village apartment she shared with two other girls when she first came
to New York. It is a far cry from the uptown apartment
with a terrace that she shares now with Dave, her lover,
an earnest young man struggling to be a sports writer for
another New York magazine empire. They have been
living together more than a year and sharing expenses, as
well as experiences, in their highly competitive world.
Dave is hip to the ways of business in New York and does
not question Tracy about her late hours and the occasional
nights when she doesn't come home at all.

"Tracy is in a high-pressure operation. When she's
working on a project—getting one of the magazine's authors on a talk show or something like that—I appreciate
what it takes, what she feels she has to do. I trust her to
do what's right for herself and for us," Dave says. "It may
mean that she has to put out for some creep on the production staff of some TV show. That's business. I understand. I know that if the situation were reversed, Tracy
would be just as understanding. Only thing is, I don't
know anybody who's interested in having sex with a
sports writer."

While there is an understanding between Tracy and
Dave, they make it a point never to discuss the arrangements that Tracy has to make to do her job. Nor do they
discuss any of the arrangements Tracy made during that
part of her career before she met Dave. "The past has
nothing to do with Dave and me," Tracy states confidently, her pert jaw set defiantly.

The past is, as dime-fiction writers used to say, scarlet.
The first time she used her very considerable charms to

further her career was in college. In deep trouble in a class for which numerous papers were required that she had not written ("I was having a terribly torrid affair with a Harvard boy at the time," she notes), Tracy pitched her professor a proposition that the man chose to accept. She wiped out her classroom deficiencies in a cottage on a wintry weekend in Rockport, Massachusetts. "It was very out of the way, very safe, and very cold," Tracy explains. "I also got an A."

Taking a job with a small public-relations outfit in Boston, Tracy was a general gal Friday, but she soon learned that her job also involved duty on Saturdays and Sundays and overnight during the week. "I was there primarily to entertain clients," she recalls. "The job paved the way to New York."

Part of her present responsibility is to arrange various parties and entertainments for those doing business with her employer. These people include authors, advertisers, advertising-agency people, and occasionally a celebrity who is being featured in the magazine.

She finds the job exciting. It pays very well. She is not sure if she and Dave will get married. "That remains to be seen," she explains. "If it happens, okay. And what about the future as far as my career goes? Well, the day will probably come when what I have to offer in the area of public relations and publicity isn't all that exciting. If that happens, I have an ace up my sleeve. Back in high school I learned some secretarial skills. I'm a whiz at shorthand. And I type as well as any gal down in the pool. There's always a spot for a secretary."

And there is always room for a good recommendation. An executive of a medium-sized tool-making company was looking for a new executive secretary. While on a business trip to the Southwest, he mentioned his need to a prospective client. "I'll find you a nice secretary," said the client. True to his word, the client referred a young woman to the office of the tool executive. "She was a gorgeous girl," the tool executive notes, "and she said she was only looking for a hundred and thirty dollars a week salary. Well, the deal was simple. My company would pay her the hundred and thirty dollars, but the client in the Southwest would pay her also. It was his way of getting the contract we had been talking about. I made the deal. She happens to be a fine executive secretary, I might point out."

While the legendary casting couch is still a going concern in show business, it has become common in other areas of American business, but there are often rigid ground rules to keep office sex within the confines of the executive suite. A young mailroom boy was recently fired by a large New York corporation because he indiscreetly stated that he would like to have intercourse with one of the office girls, yet a young executive of that firm encountered no difficulty with the morals clause of his employment contract after he alternately squeezed, pinched, and pawed that same girl at a cocktail party in full view of the top executives of the company. These top executives lay down strict rules of conduct for their employees, while they pad expense accounts, keep clandestine second apartments, hire call girls, and sanction the use of sex to win contracts. The inhabitants of the executive suite guard their prerogatives jealously.

Knowing where the skeletons are hidden has been the secret of success for many a sojourner in the upper echelons of American business, and few of those sojourners know more than the gals who go to work daily armed with steno pad and sharpened pencil.

The director of personnel for a corporation headquartered in Atlanta, Georgia, has spent nearly a lifetime observing the habits of people who want to get ahead in business, especially women. "There are certain girls in lower or middle management ranks that feel that sex contact is very important for their growth within a company," he notes. "These gals take advantage of their sex and offer it around rather freely. You get these cold-blooded, ambitious kids who couldn't care less what they do as long as they get where they want to go. When you look at a personnel record and see a lot of movement by a girl who isn't all that great, frankly, you know something is going on. Women in business are extremely interesting. They are not usually motivated by the things that motivate the men. A man wants a promotion in order to put more money in his pocket. With many women the money is secondary. Ego is involved. They seem to feel that they have something to prove. You know, a lot of women get satisfaction in knowing that men have to report to them."

Until a young woman reaches the heady heights of the top echelons of American business, her plight is hard, and sometimes the poor working girl has to pick up an odd job or two on the outside. The opportunities are vast, indeed.

2
Donna

"How would you like to triple your income?"

Donna looked up from her work, blinked her beautiful blue eyes, and said, "Sure. Who wouldn't?" She went immediately back to her work collating pages for a script to be used in the filming of a TV commercial the next day. As a production secretary she was expected to do such menial work, but she also had the chance to be in the studio when the filming was done. Films were Donna's great passion. The production of them fascinated her. She had no interest in acting, although she was an attractive girl to whom such offers had been made. Wholesome, freckled, and healthy, she could have played the role of the All-American girl easily. But she was also seductive in a June Allyson way. Her oval face was pretty, her eyes bright blue, her teeth straight, her breasts full and firm and lifted. Tending to be heavy in the hips and thighs, she watched her diet closely. But production, not acting, was her interest, and she had settled for a low-paying job to be part of a production team. This job gave her $75 a week take-home pay.

"I'm not kidding about a chance to triple what you earn," said the questioner.

"Is this another pitch to get me to go to lunch?" she laughed.

"Strictly business. Over lunch if you like."

"Are you paying?"

"I'm paying."

Donna didn't know it, but her life was about to change dramatically and in a way that she would never have expected. Donna was about to be asked if she wanted to become an executive prostitute.

She shuddered at the word. Even "call girl" sounded crass, hard, and repulsive to her. Donna was 25 years of age, single, and the daughter of a middle-class Jewish family. She had been raised by a moral code that counted prostitution as an evil. Even premarital sexual relations were taboo in the moral strictures taught her by her parents. Those mores held for Donna until she was in college, an exclusive women's institution in the Northeast. Her first sexual intercourse occurred as part of a deeply felt love affair when she was a junior. Feelings of guilt haunted her at first, but she was able to reconcile her actions with her upbringing. College and work in New York City liberalized much of that upbringing, but her views on prostitution remained intact.

"Girls just like you are earning up to five hundred dollars a week," she was told.

"I don't think I could do it," she replied.

"Why don't you have a talk with this madam I know? At least keep an open mind about it. You could use the money."

"I can always use money," Donna laughed.

"Think about it."

"Okay," she said, expecting to dismiss the entire proposition from her thoughts as soon as she finished her lunch. But a week later she found herself confronted with it once more.

"I can set up a meeting for you with the madam," she was told. "What do you say?"

"When do I have to let you know?" Donna said, more out of a desire to be polite than anything else.

"Tomorrow."

The next day Donna was still ambivalent about the prospect of meeting a madam and talking about prostitution. But she was a curious girl if nothing else, and she had never met a madam before. "I'll talk to her, sure," she announced.

The meeting was arranged.

The madam was an impressive woman. Elegantly dressed in clothes that were quietly understated but obviously expensive, she was a woman in her thirties with a trim figure, proud carriage, and a gentle, pleasant voice. She invited Donna into an apartment on New York's Upper East Side. Its windows looked out on the East River. Done in a mixture of modern and Oriental furnishings, the apartment impressed Donna with its opulence. She was not aware of a feeling of sin or decadence. She felt rather comfortable.

"I'm glad you took the time to come up and visit," the woman said with a smile. "Would you like a drink?"

"A soft drink if you have one."

The woman smiled and touched Donna lightly on the hand. "Of course."

In a moment the madam presented Donna with a tall, cold glass of Coke. With the grace of an actress the madam sank into a large leather chair across the room from the young woman and lifted a drink to her own lips. "Scotch," she said with a lilting voice. Setting the glass down, she waited a moment, letting the Coke and the interval put Donna at ease. When she felt the moment and the mood were right, she drew back the veil that obscures the world of executive prostitution.

MADAM: First let me give you a sketch of the sort of business I'm involved in. Then you can ask all the questions I'm sure you have in mind. I am a madam. I have three or four girls who work for me. The girls average twenty-five to fifty dollars per trick. Laid and leave. If somebody wants a party or dinner or show, that will be from fifty to a hundred dollars. Once you became associated with us, you would receive half and I would receive half. Of course, all this is in cash. Our clients are usually businessmen, high executives. We have lawyers, government officials, top men in society and show business. The average age of the men is forty-five to fifty-five. All of them are married. I don't like to have single men. Single men create problems. I do not contact the girls at their homes. They contact me. They tell me in advance when they will be available. As a result, I'm able to know what bookings to make. I may get a call from a John— that's what we call our customers. He may call and say that he's in town and wants to come over in an hour. Do I have anybody? If I don't have anybody, I lose a job. I like to know where my girls are and when they are available. We try to get and keep the best clientele, and I try to keep them to a limited number. I like repeat business. We have a clientele now of ten, twenty, or thirty men. They may come in once a week. One fellow comes here every Tuesday night at seven o'clock. He has one girl that he likes rather than selecting different ones all the time. We do not allow any sadism or masochism. We're a straight group. I know exactly what my girls will do or won't do. The Johns know ahead of time. If they don't like it, they can leave. There is no possibility of any trouble. We are well respected in this building. We don't have boisterous parties. I'm sure you must have some questions. Ask anything you want.

DONNA: What necessitates one of these men to seek outside contact with other women? Are they having trouble in their own marriages? Is it variety? Are they trying to regain their youth?

MADAM: Usually most of the men are looking for a sympathetic ear. They do want variety in their sexual relationships. Maybe they are not even having one with their wives. What they are looking for is to get laid with no involvement. They may cry on your shoulder a bit and tell you their problems. But when the trick is over, they go, and that is it.

DONNA: What kind of girls come to you? Why do they come?

MADAM: Extra money. Some are housewives. Most are middle class. I've met a lot of girls whom I've had to turn away because they were streetwalkers and wanted to get into a call-girl operation. I don't think they fit in. If our clients wanted streetwalkers, they could go out on the streets to get them. I maintain a very clean house. I make sure my girls are clean. I've never had a girl come down with any kind of disease.

DONNA: Of all the girls you've had working for you, have any of them had any psychological problems adjusting to what they are doing?

MADAM: No. The thing is, what they are doing, no one is forcing them to do. You want to walk out the door, you can walk out the door.

DONNA: It's not that I mean forcing necessarily, but suppose a girl might feel that this might be an interesting experience, that it might be a way of making extra money that is needed—

MADAM: That is the reason most girls give.

DONNA: Right, I assume that's the basic motivation. Then say a girl would try it for a week or longer, have any girls in that situation ever had a serious hang-up about what they were doing? Did they resolve it? Or did they just stop doing what they were doing? Did they feel guilty?

MADAM: No, as a matter of fact, I had several girls that worked here for a short period of time, the first time they had worked as prostitutes. There was one girl who worked here for a month. She had a boy friend, and they became engaged. She was going to stop hooking, and she did for a while. She got married. I didn't see her for a while. Then one day she called and said she decided to come back. She said she didn't have any psychological hang-ups at all. In fact, she felt the experience added to her marriage because she was totally aware of how to please her husband.

DONNA: Was her husband aware of what she was doing?

MADAM: She never told her husband.

DONNA: When she went back, she didn't tell him?

MADAM: No. She had resolved it within herself. She told her husband she had a job.

DONNA: Did she have any fears her husband would find out?

MADAM: No. She felt that she could explain it.

DONNA: She did? That's interesting. She felt she could justify what she was doing?

MADAM: Exactly.

DONNA: Who takes the precautions as far as birth control?

MADAM: What do you do for birth control?

DONNA: I have been on the Pill, although I've had trouble and have been off and on, so that would be it, the Pill.

MADAM: Most Johns don't like to be asked to use a condom. They would prefer that you take the precaution, not them.

DONNA: What would be the average amount of money that could be made in a week?

MADAM: Let's start off in a different way. A lot has to do with your personality. I'd be willing to start off by making you a fifty-dollar girl, which means we split it. Now, depending on the hours that you are available, I can guarantee you one or two tricks a day, which might be one and a half to two hours of work. Say you work five days a week. That's part-time and wouldn't take you late into the evening.

DONNA: Oh, that would be on an evening basis.

MADAM: Well, if you were available in the afternoon, the same thing. I assume you have a job and want to maintain that job, at least while you are trying this out. If you decide to go full-time, then you could make four to five hundred dollars a week, working just days. If you wanted to work even longer hours, you could make as much as eight hundred to a thousand dollars weekly.

DONNA: Talking big money.

MADAM: Oh yes, we're talking big clients. We're not talking about a guy that picks up girls off the street. You have to understand that there is a big difference. We're a call-girl operation.

DONNA: Are the girls known by their real names?

MADAM: Any name you want.

DONNA: In other words, there would be no reason for a man to know my real name?

MADAM: None whatsoever. Nobody would ever have to know your real name. I don't even have to know it.

DONNA: Okay. There's never been a problem with men getting emotionally involved with any of the girls?

MADAM: No. If you find that someone is getting too familiar, you can just let me know and I'll see that you and he are not put together again.

DONNA: Are there any mirrors or anything like that?

MADAM: No. We have straight sex. I'm talking about intercourse and fellatio. That would be the only requirement. If you have something that you don't want to do, let me know. In other words, if you feel that you would not want a man to ejaculate in your mouth, tell me, and I'll be sure that you get Johns who are not interested in that. Naturally, the more you do, the more clients there are and the more money you'll make.

DONNA: Are the girls that work for you friendly with each other?

MADAM: That's up to you.

DONNA: Here's something I have thought about—having been in the position of going to bed with a man I've had some degree of feeling for, how does one cope with going to bed with someone one may not have any physical attraction for, going further than that, have physical revulsion for?

MADAM: The only thing that I can tell you is that you have to be as open-minded as possible. You don't line the Johns up and pick out the ones you want. You are going to find that prostitutes have to be the best actresses in the world. You can treat it as a game, as a matter of fact. If a John knows, or thinks, that you are having an orgasm with him, he's going to want to come back to see you again. Obviously you're not going to have an orgasm every time.

DONNA: I'm not even getting as far as having an orgasm. I'm worried about being stimulated in the initial sense. What does a girl do who is so physically revolted or repelled by a man that she can go almost into a frigid state at the prospect of being in bed with him and couldn't possibly respond and lubricate or anything like that? How can a girl handle a situation like that?

MADAM: Most girls can accept the fact that they are being professional. We hope that you just don't get into bed with a guy and make him have intercourse right away. We hope that when he comes in that he'll sit down and have a drink. The music will be on. You will treat him as a gentleman, and in turn, he will treat you as a lady. You're giving him something he wants, and he knows that. He's going to treat you the way you should be treated. He's not going to be an animal.

DONNA: I have this idea that any man that would utilize the services of a prostitute would feel that she is just a piece of merchandise. All right, she's a woman and you'd be a little more careful with a woman than a set of golf clubs, but do you think these men respect these women?

MADAM: I believe they do. That's been my experience. We're people, after all. The girls that work here are very sincere. We are not out to take a guy for anything.

DONNA: Yet the kind of respect that a man would have for you or for any of your girls would certainly not be the same kind of respect he has for his wife. I guess I still haven't accepted the idea that sex is something to be sold.

MADAM: How many men have you slept with?

DONNA: In my life?

MADAM: Yes.

DONNA: Probably less than ten.

MADAM: Now, each one of those I assume was an emotional involvement. Did you ever sleep with any of those men on the first night you went out with them?

DONNA: No.

MADAM: After you did go to bed with one of them and, let's say, the next morning he sent you a gift. How would you treat that?

DONNA: I get the point.

MADAM: You resolved it, right?

DONNA: I would say the first two times it was kind of difficult for me to accept, and I think I accepted it in the sense that I kind of divorced myself from myself much as I'm doing in this conversation with you. Of the ten men, I really only had a deep emotional involvement with one.

MADAM: So the other nine could have paid you?

DONNA: In a way, I guess that's true.

MADAM: Can I ask you, during the sexual experiences you've had, were they all sexually satisfying to you?

DONNA: No, as a matter of fact, one of my major hang-ups is that I don't think I ever had an orgasm before I met and slept with the man I'm in love with right now. It doesn't happen all the time, but he makes me happy whether I achieve orgasm or not. That to me is of prime consideration in deciding what I'm going to do from here. My relationship with him is very important. I'm very much afraid that if I were to prostitute myself with other men that it would affect my relationship with him, in terms of guilt feelings.

MADAM: I've found that doesn't happen. It didn't happen to me.

DONNA: Do your other girls have boy friends?

MADAM: Some do.

DONNA: I assume the boy friends don't know what the girls are doing.

MADAM: One of them does. He has accepted it.

DONNA: I have to admit that it's a very enticing kind of thing, certainly monetarily. I need the money.

MADAM: There are a lot of things you would like to have.

DONNA: The money would be nice, and yet what would I do to explain my sudden wealth?

MADAM: Nobody would have to know. An extra job. Savings.

DONNA: Lie about it. Cover up for myself. I remember my father telling me I should never lie because you have to remember your stories, and sooner or later you'll be caught. My boy friend is very bright. I think he'd get suspicious. That's what bothers me. My relationship with him. If I didn't have that, I might just jump right into this.

MADAM: Try it and see what happens.

DONNA: Once you're in, you're in.

MADAM: Not at all. Why do you say that?

DONNA: Because you've done it. When you really come down to the nitty-gritty, you're talking about me going against everything I've been brought up to believe in. I know the attractions. I could really use the money. There may be interesting men to meet. I could probably learn something from these men. On the other hand, I've been brought up not to do this sort of thing. One part of me says

I shouldn't get involved. Another says to try it just for the—

MADAM: Adventure.

DONNA: Adventure.

MADAM: Did you ever think of asking your boy friend what his reaction might be?

DONNA: Well, knowing that I was going to meet you and talk about this, the whole idea has been very much on my mind. But on the way over here I was sure that I was ninety percent decided not to do it. Now, I think I'm swinging the other way. If you said you had someone in the other room, I just might do it.

MADAM: Then, why don't you?

DONNA: The curiosity factor alone is enough to make me want to do it. At this point I'm afraid of the actual act.

MADAM: I will make sure the first person is someone I know, someone with whom I know you wouldn't have anything to worry about. A gentleman.

DONNA: I've always been a flirt. I love men. I'd ten times rather be with men than women.

MADAM: If you love men, then this is the right profession.

DONNA: Please don't keep saying profession. I'd rather say avocation.

MADAM: Do you feel that you are prepared to try it right now?

DONNA: I would really like to think about it. I think the further I get away from this conversation the more I will be against doing it. I really should give it some thought. Would that be okay?

MADAM: That is entirely up to you. You know where you can find me.

DONNA: I hope I haven't wasted your time.

MADAM: Not at all. I just want to say finally that if you love men, this is the, uh, avocation that could bring you enjoyment and money to have some of the things in life that you want and you deserve. You let me know, okay?

DONNA: Okay.

Outside, a cold rain was falling but Donna ignored the weather and walked across town to her apartment. Entering it, she turned on the lights and was struck by the bareness of the room, its dreariness compared to the comfortable opulence of the apartment she had just left. Taking off her coat and hanging it in her only closet, she paused and fondled her small wardrobe. In a year she had been able to buy herself only two new dresses. There had been a sale at one of the big department stores. She realized that whenever she bought anything it was because someone was having a sale. She considered calling her boy friend, but it was late and she decided against phoning. She went to bed, but it was a long time before she slept. In the morning she awoke convinced that she had made the right decision.

"How did it go last night?" she was asked at work by the person who had arranged her interview with the madam.

"I decided against it," she said flatly.

"Well, to each his own. If you change your mind, I'm sure you'd be welcome over there."

"I won't be changing my mind," she said confidently.

Ultimately, events changed her mind for her. The grim news came in a notice on the bulletin board:

DUE TO THE ECONOMIC SLUMP, IT WILL BE NECESSARY FOR THE AGENCY TO CUT BACK ITS PERSONNEL. THOSE AFFECTED BY THIS UNHAPPY TURN OF EVENTS WILL BE NOTIFIED BY LETTER IN THEIR NEXT PAYCHECKS.

Donna's letter was quite direct. Her job was being eliminated, and her work would be taken over by the producers.

Three weeks later, after looking for jobs that did not exist or for which she was "overqualified," Donna confronted a collection of bills for which she had no money. Neither her small savings account, unemployment benefits, nor one free-lance script-editing job amounted to the sum she needed for rent and other debts then due. The total due was modest, less than $300, but it was far beyond her means. "That was the grim prospect," she recalled, "as I sat at my kitchen table one evening—the night before the rent was due—and added up everything I owed. I sat there trying to figure out how to raise that kind of money, and all the while, in the back of my mind, I knew where I could get it. I tried to sleep that night but just tossed and turned. I phoned that certain number the next morning."

"I can have something for you this afternoon and, if you desire, a couple of dates this evening," said the cheerful yet sympathetic voice of the madam on the phone.

"He was an older man," Donna told the authors. "A businessman of some kind, not from New York. I guess he knew what the situation was with me. He was very kind."

Over drinks Donna and the John chatted about inconsequential things—the weather, the excitements of New York, how good the Scotch was. The conversation was difficult and filled with long pauses. Donna clasped her glass tightly, sipped from it nervously. When the John put his hand on her thigh, she nearly spilled her drink. "I'm sorry," she said, trying to smile.

"I'm just as nervous as you are," the John chuckled.

The way he said it put Donna more at ease. She looked at the man more closely. He was most distinguished in appearance. His brown hair was heavily laced with gray and was completely gray at the temples. His brows were thick but dark. His eyes were green, flecked with brown, and gentle. He had a wide, firm mouth and a strong jaw with no double chin. His hand on her thigh was warm, even through her skirt, strong but kind. As his hand crept upward along her thigh, she sipped her drink again, draining it, and was startled by the cold bump of an ice cube against her nose. At the same time the John's hand slid between her legs and pressed into her flesh. She closed her eyes and then felt his parted, moist lips against her cheek. "Shall we go to bed?" he whispered.

Donna rose, straightened her skirt, and walked as calmly as she could to the bed. She sat upon it and took off her shoes. The John stood in a corner of the large bedroom tugging at his necktie. Donna diverted her eyes from him and proceeded to remove all of her clothes. Naked, she quickly slipped under the covers of the king-size bed. The John was getting out of his shorts, and as he turned toward her, Donna stared at him, her eyes fixed on his erection. He came to the bed and got under the covers with her. His feet were cold, but his hands cupping her breasts were warm and moist.

Pushing down the covers and baring her breasts, the John bent over them, kissing each. Then his hands moved down; she held her breath and closed her eyes, lying absolutely still. Working gently but insistently, he caressed her, jolting her into spasmodic, frenzied response. She laid her hands on his head, stroking him, tangling her fingers in his hair. He responded immediately to her touch and caressed her wildly, hungrily, ceaselessly until she nearly sobbed with excitement.

Suddenly he loomed above her, his face as large as a close-up on a movie screen. He smiled. His eyes were misty. "Everything okay?" he whispered. She nodded and managed her own small smile. Then she felt him against her; he paused, holding her shoulders in his large hands. She felt little of his weight as he rested above her gentlemanly on his elbows and knees. Slowly and considerately, he moved, taking his time, keeping his eyes upon hers, smiling from time to time and occasionally kissing her lightly, almost fatherly, on her forehead. Presently the movements quickened. Sensing his approaching climax, she responded, working against him, helping him. It was over quickly then. They lingered for a time, lying side by side, and then he dressed, kissed her, thanked her, and left.

Returning to her apartment that night, Donna had enough money for her rent. Within six months she had moved into a new apartment where she lives with her boy friend.

"He was very understanding when I told him what I was doing," she told the authors as she sat in her apartment, her boy friend at her side. "I had to tell, of course. At the moment I'm a call girl. We have both adjusted to it. We each know it's temporary. When we get married, it will stop."

She reached out to him. They held hands. It seemed a remarkably innocent gesture.

3
". . . Everything but computers."

"I never forgot that I was in business," wrote Polly Adler in her memoirs *A House is Not a Home*, a fascinating account of Polly's reign as the queen of New York madams in the heyday of Prohibition.

"The modern madam had better not forget that she is in business, either," says a madam of today.

Meet Rose!

Near Madison Square Garden along a street lined by high-rise luxury apartments is Rose's place. From the outside it is like all the other buildings, and her apartment on a floor near the top of the building is modest compared to some that Rose has known and that she could easily afford today. It is an apartment with a large living room, a kitchen, a dining alcove, and a bedroom with adjoining bathroom. The décor is modern; the furnishings are few but elegant. Two huge couches dominate the living room and flank an impressive stereo and accompanying record collection. The music is soft, lush, romantic. The couches are convertibles. The carpet is wall-to-wall. A telephone is always handy.

Rose runs an operation of six to twelve girls out of this apartment, and her clients are strictly the best: a judge, two assistant district attorneys, doctors, corporation executives, and a scattering of show-business personalities. Each has been approved by Rose before he ever sets foot into her establishment.

Just under 30, Rose has recognized that her own days as a call girl are almost over. She adjusts. Trim of figure, tall, poised, and practiced in her manners and mannerisms, she watches her diet as closely as she watches her bank accounts. Her clothes are understated. Her jewelry is sparse but real. When she's doing her bookwork, she finds that glasses help. When she is the hostess, the glasses are put away. In a few years she could be cast in anybody's production of *Auntie Mame*. Today, she likes the role she plays: "Madam of the best and most exclusive service in this city!"

The key to her operation is the telephone. "Everything is done on the phone," she says, waving her ringed fingers toward the phones in her apartment. Just as crucial to the operation are the listings of clients. "First of all, you have to get your books together. You have to be able to sit there at the telephone for six hours and make money lining up Johns, otherwise you won't be able to get chicks to work for you. Then there are certain people in the city that you call for girls. You call these people, and you interview these chicks. Then you go from there. You set up the hours, so many hours a day. A John comes up, does his thing, and leaves. To take care of him, I have a business that has everything but computers."

Rose puts as much value in the way a young woman speaks as the way she looks physically. "Some girls sound like street whores," she says with disgust. "They won't do for the men I service."

Fees have changed over the years, Rose points out. "It started out a sixty-forty cut. The girls would get sixty and the madam, forty. Now it has gone to half-and-half because the cost of living has gone up. Besides, I feel the madam should be making the fifty percent because she's taking all the risk. Her house is going to be closed down, she's going to go to jail, she's going to lose the money. The cut is going to go to sixty-forty again, but this time the madam will be getting the sixty and the girl, forty. Inflation is the reason. Costs of everything have gone up. You have no idea what I spend each week just for linen service. We use a lot of towels, you know." Rose estimates that she earns between $100 and $150 a day on the present fifty-fifty share of the fees collected from Johns.

Unlike some madams who maintain two apartments—one for business and one for their home—Rose uses her apartment as her residence and her place of business. "Some girls really go all-out for plush apartments, but to do that you've got to have an almost exclusively high-paying clientele. In that high bracket you've got to serve liquor, and that costs a lot of money. Johns can wreck an apartment. They're paying their money, and they feel they can do what they want. You can't risk offending them."

Rose talks bitterly about the rise of swingers' groups because she feels they have cut into her business. "A John will try to get into a swing so he can save the money. Girls in swings are not hookers. They're having sex for free. Hooking houses have been doing poorly. But someday these gals who are doing it for free will start demanding money, and the swing thing will drop off.

"There's just too much money to be made in this business for anyone to be giving sex away for free," she laughs. "What's more, a lot of girls are going to be turned on by the glamour that surrounds this business. There is a certain glamour about it, plus the added benefits of the hours you work and the exciting people you meet. There's a lot of room for new ideas, too."

When asked if she ever considered issuing credit cards, as was done in 1968 by an innovative group in Chicago, she replied, "Credit cards? That might not be a bad idea." The Chicago operation allegedly handled $300,000 a month in business. Four men were convicted of using the mail to promote prostitution. Prostitute Alma Smith testified that the men mailed credit cards to more than 6,000 men inviting them to a house of prostitution in Chicago.

Rose's house is far from opulent compared to some that have operated in other cities, including New York. In June 1968, police closed down a lavish brothel that a New York detective described as resembling a Roman orgy. "It was a social event and a home away from home," stated Attorney Harold O. N. Frankel when he appeared in criminal court to defend the girls arrested at the establishment. Located on Lexington Avenue in an exclusive neighborhood, the house was a four-story brownstone containing two living rooms and five bedrooms. A swimming pool and sauna were in the basement as well as table tennis and billiard equipment. The house catered to businessmen visiting New York City. The police found out about the plush operation from an outraged visitor who had been invited there with the understanding that there was to be a party. When the raid occurred, some patrons were swimming in the pool. They reportedly fled without their clothes.

Yet even the house on Lexington Avenue paled in comparison to the legendary operations under the auspices of Lucky Luciano in 1936. Known as the "vice czar," Luciano still holds the record for running the biggest prostitution racket in the city's history. Writing about the colorful Lucky, *New York Times* reporter J. Anthony

Lukas said: "Luciano worked through such 'bookers' as Cockeye Louis Weiner and Warren (Little Caesar) Mims, who for ten dollars a week per girl provided protection to such madams as Cokey Flo Brown, French Irene and Dago Jean. He made prostitution pay handsomely until former District Attorney Thomas E. Dewey put him away for thirty to fifty years."

Since Luciano's heyday prostitution has been far less organized and considerably less colorful. There have been exceptions, as in the case of oleo heir Minot Frazier (Mickey) Jelke III who was arrested in a café-society vice scandal in 1952.

Lukas, in his 1967 survey of prostitution for the *Times*, quoted a madam named Rhoda. "The little gray-haired old madam you used to see sitting in the parlor—she's gone now. The old type went out with the brothel. There aren't more than a dozen real houses left in the city and most of them are in Harlem. Many call girls who used to work for a madam ten years ago are madams themselves today."

Rose was once a call girl, and although she may turn an occasional trick herself today, she regards those days as over. "I have other girls working for me. I run the business," she states emphatically.

Business of her sort may often require payoffs for protection, but because Rose has so many important clients —judges and men from the district attorney's office—she feels that paying protection to the police is not necessary. She is atypical. Most madams do pay for protection, although some more courageous ones are insulted by the idea. In 1971 a madam who felt that she was being persecuted by a New York detective turned him in. The 16-year veteran of the force was arrested for allegedly attempting to extort $400 from the madam, who operated a house on the Upper East Side. The madam who blew the whistle was not prosecuted. Another madam walked into another New York City precinct station a few years ago and handed the desk sergeant the badge and gun of a cop who she said had refused to pay for the services she provided. That cop was also prosecuted. The President's Commission on Law Enforcement and Administration of Justice, Task Force Report on Organized Crime, 1967, noted one police operation that "tolerated all prostitutes who kept up their protection payments." The study cited a madam who controlled more than 20 girls. The madam paid $500 a week for protection. Another madam with only one girl working for her paid $75 a week. The task force noted that most policemen "began to ignore prostitution and gambling" after their reports of these activities were reported without action to superiors.

While Rose has a stable of six to twelve girls working for her, she can, if the need arises, deal with a broker. These people maintain lists—nationwide in scope—of women available for work as call girls. "They send them to you at a ten-percent commission," Rose points out. She does not often feel the need to call a broker. "There is an unlimited supply of girls, so I don't have any trouble getting girls to work for me."

She is scrupulous about two things—health and drugs. "I don't allow drugs here. If I have any sign that they are drug users, they have to go. I run a clean house. I also make sure that my girls see a doctor once a week. I want a clean house, so no drugs and there must be regular checkups."

The health checks start immediately. "Girls have to come to me with a doctor's slip. *My doctor.* My doctor will not allow anyone to come to me unless she is clean. I know he won't send me anyone who is not clean. When I know that a girl is clean, I can stand behind her. If a John complains that he got something here, I send him to my doctor, discreetly, and the doctor assures the guy that he didn't get his problem at my house. As far as the girls go,

I call the doctor after their checkups and get his report directly. I make sure I get checkups myself, too."

An intelligent, sophisticated woman with good taste in clothes, food, and other aspects of her life, Rose is also a woman who is wise to the world. Nothing can surprise her. No desire shocks her. She has heard of every kind of sexual taste and witnessed most of them. Her business is to cater to them.

"There's nothing new under the sun when it comes to sex," says Rose, "not even the electric vibrators that've got everybody turned on. They've been in use since the thirties, actually. There are some modifications, but the principle is the same as those massagers that barbers and masseurs have been using all these years and the hip people have been using in their bedrooms just as long. Trouble is, you can get addicted to those things."

Rose has not yet been converted to the idea of installing a waterbed in her house. "A lot of my friends have told me that they're out of this world when it comes to balling, but I keep having this vision of all that water suddenly pouring out all over the place."

Occasionally she is asked to set up a party for a group of men, including a sex show. "Mostly it's just a case of two of the girls making it with each other. That turns on a lot of men apparently. Anyway, I have two lovely gals who dig each other, and they put on quite a show. I had one John here some time back who said he wanted those girls to teach him cunnilingus, so I set up this little informal class. He was a very bright student."

Schooling in the arts of sexual pleasure has become part of Rose's business. She is thinking about writing a book on sexual technique based on the classes she has given on how to make love to a woman, how to please a man, and how to provide the satisfaction that is sought by people who are deeply enmeshed in various sexual deviations.

On a hot summer evening Rose conducted a class in S

and M (the shorthand for sadism-masochism), the art of extracting sexual excitement and pleasure from the inflicting of pain or humiliation or the receiving of it. For the class, Rose assembled three of her new call girls, three male clients, and a young man and woman as demonstrators of the arts. Also in attendance, one of the authors posed as Rose's bodyguard. The Johns according to Rose were a lawyer, a writer, and a vice president of an advertising firm in Chicago. The class was held in Rose's apartment. For it, the couches had been pushed against the wall. A large, low table stood against another wall. On it were arrayed some of the implements used in S and M— an assortment of dildoes, a small leather whip, rope, a dog collar and leash, three sets of handcuffs, and a variety of leather straps and thongs. She toys with these items as she delivers the opening remarks in her lecture on the special S and M arts. The little talk is punctuated with chuckles and laughter. Rose tries to keep it light because the subject itself is heavy.

"I find that the most prominent people are the worst ones when it comes to being weird, wanting to tie you up, the whole bit," she begins. "They've got everything that money can buy, and now they are not satisfied with being normal. They have to be freakier. They have the bread to pay for deviations."

She taps a leather whip against her hip and flashes a wide smile. Privately she admits, "S and M cracks me up. I think it's funny. I don't know how anyone can enjoy it."

To the class, she relates some of the things that can be expected:

ROSE: Some guys like to be dominated. You have to put a leash on them and make them crawl around the floor. They love it. You know, kiss my feet, lick my toes. I had a guy turn on me one time, but fortunately I was smart enough to handle it. There was another John who was into a sadist bag. He wanted to dominate. He kept saying he was going to tie me up and do it to me until one day I got fed up and said to him, "Oh, shut up. I can't stand your big mouth." And do you know something? He turned into a pussycat. After that I turned the whole thing around, and I was the dominant one. I used to send him on the street with a coat on but no clothes underneath to get a pack of cigarettes or something. He used to love it. Another time I was on the phone, and he was in the room. I turned to him and said, "By the time I get off this phone, you'd better come because I don't want to waste my time with you." He used to freak out and love it. This guy was a two-hundred-dollar John. He paid by the hour. He paid a hundred dollars an hour. He had it. He's a very notorious John in New York City. I think every whore in town knows this guy.

The class continues as Rose turns to the specifics of how to serve men like the ones she described. She shows the use of the whip. "It's all in the wrist," she solemnly points out. She painstakingly relates what a girl can be expected to know and to do, the difference between dominating and being dominated, the things a masochist likes to hear, and the words a sadist likes uttered while he is performing his special sexual games. While these encounters could be dangerous, Rose feels, and many psychologists agree, that sadism and masochism is really a game, one that often involves little more than masturbation at the end of the fantasy that has been enacted. "You've got to take it all very casually," Rose concludes her lecture. "It is a game."

Rose also assures the members of the class that the clients who visit her house with an inclination toward S and M have been carefully screened to eliminate those who might regard their sadomasochistic adventures as more than games.

Rose is a student of her profession. She quotes often

from the autobiography of Polly Adler, New York's most famous madam. While the days of legendary whore-mistresses such as Polly Adler are gone, Rose feels that she, like Polly Adler before her, is a necessity. She offers a service to men who find, for whatever reason, that they are being shut out by their own wives. Rose takes down her dog-eared paperback copy of Polly Adler's book, flips it open to an obviously well-read passage, and reads it aloud*:

"Why shouldn't a man turn from such a wife to my girls, who were always beautifully groomed and lovely to look at and gay and responsive, who were always flattering him, sympathizing with him, telling him what a terrific lover he was? Of course they were getting paid for it, but doesn't a wife get paid too? It is not a new point of view, but so far as I'm concerned a prostitute is anyone who sells herself for gain. The women who take husbands not out of love but out of greed, to get their bills paid, to get a fine house and clothes and jewels; the women who marry to get out of a tiresome job, or to get away from disagreeable relatives, or to avoid being called an old maid—these are whores in everything but name. The only difference between them and my girls is that my girls gave a man his money's worth."

*From *A House is Not a Home* by Polly Adler.

4

Prostitute Payola

"Here I am horny as hell and stuck in this goddamned crosstown traffic," grumbled Randy Macum, a lanky, easygoing young man with a reputation as the most important time buyer in radio. He stared a moment at the immobilized traffic clogging the street, shook his head, then looked to his side at the time salesman of one of the biggest radio stations in the city. "These cars are welded together, I think," Randy said, managing a smile.

"We could walk it from here. The place is only two blocks away," said the salesman, a short, dumpy, nervous man several years Randy Macum's senior.

Randy gave an affirmative slap to his knee, and the salesman paid their cab driver. They hiked the two blocks, entered a high-rise apartment house, and took the elevator to the penthouse. There they were greeted by a buxom, grinning, bleached-blonde woman. "I'm Stella," she announced.

"Sorry we're late, Stell," said the sweating salesman, "but the traffic is fierce. This is Randy."

The woman clasped Randy's long hand in her plump and chilly ones. "Welcome," she said with a hearty laugh.

"Take good care of Randy," the salesman said, turning to leave. "He's one of my best clients."

Randy ignored the comment and looked beyond Stella at a statuesque young woman lolling on a couch across the living room of the penthouse. Long red hair cascaded to her shoulders, which were bared by a plunging V-neckline dress that revealed the smooth texture of a pair of the largest and most inviting breasts Randy had ever seen. He stared.

"Meet Carlotta," said Stella, turning and waving her arm toward the distant figure. "Your date for the afternoon."

Carlotta rose and crossed the room. Her legs were long and firm, her hips, broad and rocking provocatively. She stood close to Randy and put her arms around his waist. "Hi," she said, kissing him on the mouth.

Stella stood by a door to a bedroom as Randy and Carlotta passed through it. She closed it slowly and quietly and crossed to a desk in a corner of the living room and went about the business of being a madam, noting in her ledger book that this visit by Randy Macum had earned her credit with the radio station for an expensive AM-FM portable radio—a gift for her nephew.

Stella, one of the savviest madams working today, had accepted a rather revolutionary business proposal made on behalf of the radio station that had sent Randy Macum to her. For providing girls for clients of the station, Stella in turn would receive merchandise from the radio station's supply of goods delivered to it in payment for commercials. No money changed hands. It was strictly barter. Stella liked the arrangement very much.

In the bedroom Randy Macum thought the arrangement was fine. Lying naked in bed, his head cradled in his hands, Randy pondered for a moment the genius who had devised such a splendid way to bribe him into giving the station the very substantial advertising business that he controlled as a time buyer. His admiration for the scheme slipped from his mind as Carlotta worked her own special wonders. At last, when Randy took her into his arms, guiding her onto her back and rising above her, he gave no further thought to how he had been bribed through this arrangement of prostitute payola but concentrated his every thought and movement on the woman whose voluptuous body enveloped him.

More than a decade ago the Federal Communications Commission discovered that bribery—payola—was common in broadcasting. Disc jockeys took money to play records on the air. Game-show hosts and producers rigged their contests. Kickbacks were common. Illicit money flowed like water. The FCC thought it had put a stop to payola.

The practice of payola is still alive and well and thriving in the broadcasting business, but it is far more sophisticated today. Payoffs now are made in merchandise, favors, and flesh—rarely money. None of it goes into account books or tax returns. Account executives, business managers, advertising sales representatives, publicity and promotion men, pimps, prostitutes, madams, and wheeling-dealing middlemen rake in TV sets, radios, stereos, furs, liquor, Caribbean vacations, and anything else that can be advertised on radio or TV. Often these dealings are not known by the very top men of broadcasting whose stations and networks benefit from the business that is channeled to them by the Madison Avenue agencies and sharp operators on station and network payrolls who make it all happen.

A general manager of a radio station in New York City beamed his pleasure at the fact that his station was "sold out" commercially in a recent month, indicating to him that the men who buy time were giving his station and its format a solid vote of confidence. In reality the men who acquired time on this station had been wined, dined, and treated to visits to one of the most exclusive bordellos in the city in an arrangement made by a member of the sales staff of the station.

Another station came under investigation by the FCC because of a questionable deal involving the supplying of merchandise for clients in a labyrinthine arrangement devised to provide payola in an almost infinite variety of ways, including sex.

These arrangements are based on what is known in broadcasting as a "trade-out." Simply, advertising time is provided by a station to a sponsor who, rather than paying cash for the time, delivers to the station a quantity of its goods equal in cash value to the cost of the air time. Appliance manufacturers, restaurants, hotels, and hundreds of other businesses dealing in goods or services make these arrangements. The stations are then able to use this warehouse of "goodies" to treat other prospective customers. Salesmen can take would-be clients to lunch using chits from a trade-out restaurant. Bonuses to salesmen can be made with merchandise—TV sets, etc.— rather than cash. Record-keeping is vague, if it exists at all, and city, state, and federal tax coffers are cheated out of their due. The trade-out is an effective and generally unpoliced tax dodge throughout the broadcasting business.

This clever device has been used to provide sexual favors to clients, salesmen, and others, and if there is reason to question the morality of these arrangements, there is certainly no reason to question the cunning of the scheme in its planning and execution.

One of the cleverest of the practitioners of the art of prostitute payola is the sales-promotion executive of a major station in New York City. This young man's system was explained to the authors by another employee of the station who acted as the middleman between the sales-promotion executive and the forward-thinking madam of one of New York's best call-girl services who saw the advantages of sex as a commodity on the trade-out arrangement. The source of this information, a young man named Danny:

DANNY: In the broadcasting business you find that a lot of media buyers at a lot of agencies are more than amenable to gratuities in all different forms, shades, and sorts— TV sets, clothing, bonus awards, incentive awards, any given commodity that the average house owner would want—including sex. There are a lot of younger media buyers that aren't as interested in sex as the older guys. Generally speaking, a guy in his late thirties and mid-forties was a ripe guy for a sexual gratuity. Now, in this particular instance, the station I worked for, the organization that was paying for the sex, had no legitimate way of paying. It was a publicly audited firm, didn't have a lot of cash to throw around; upper management in this firm wouldn't have approved of it in the first place, for whatever reasons, whether it was because they themselves were subjected to checks and balances from above and they didn't want to get involved or something else. But the lower-echelon people, the sales people, felt this was necessary. Sex was a necessary lubricant to the gears of business. Regardless of what upper management felt, upper management couldn't be hurt by what upper management didn't know. So there was no money to be given out, and this method was devised to make sex available without money changing hands. It was to be done by trade-outs. For example, if the sales-promotion guy had all the color TV sets he could use, and they had an excess of televisions in any given month, then maybe they could work out a deal with a madam that she could take one or two TVs in a trade for five or six or ten girls, depending on the quality of her material and labor and her price. Sure enough, we found a madam who was setting up a little subsidiary operation in a different part of town, and she was furnishing an apartment on a permanent basis, a permanent operational suite, so to speak, in a building that had two or three apartments like this. She came back to us and said, "All right, we'll work out a price-service ratio." For one RCA TV set, which is relatively fair-traded, an RCA console, we could be entitled to eight visits. For an RCA portable, four visits. Zenith color TV, ten visits. Large console or fur coat, ten visits. Little clothing and gift certificates of hundred-dollar denominations, one visit. There were never any complaints about her women. She had seven girls working for her. The girls she had working for her were superb. Most of them were foreign—two from Sweden, one from France, two Italian girls, one American.

AUTHORS: How did the madam work it? She got the TV?

DANNY: She got the TV set. She paid the girls in cash. She paid them the normal discount. In other words, if you visit a girl, you pay the madam fifty dollars, and she gives the girl twenty-five dollars. So, for the hundred-dollar gift certificate, it cost the madam twenty-five dollars. Of course it would depend on the product. We once had a deal with a store, and the madam didn't want the product. The store didn't carry any merchandise that the madam would ever consider wearing. There was a point where the madam called us and wanted to know if we had any carpeting. Sure enough, we were in a position to get her carpeting. So we carpeted her apartment, and for that we had credit for fifteen visits.

AUTHORS: How are these records kept?

DANNY: Strictly in people's heads. Nothing written down. The connection was between the madam and the dispenser of the goodies at the broadcast operation. He never wrote anything down. He knew in his mind how many visits—

AUTHORS: Didn't he have to account for where the merchandise was going?

DANNY: No, because the merchandise was put in the category of bribes and incentives to begin with. It was distributed to different people every month.

AUTHORS: He didn't have to answer to upper management, auditors, or his boss?

DANNY: No, he never did. Don't misunderstand me. For any given TV that left or was allocated to a person, he had to supply a name. He'd supply a name and address. Now, that name could be fictitious. Nobody cared. In addition, he dealt with agencies and the agency would give it to someone else. So you never knew who the final user was. This guy in this particular operation had seventy thousand dollars' worth of goodies to give out *every month*. Every single month.

AUTHORS: Could he usually dispose of that much?

DANNY: His "goodie closet" was more often than not, empty.

AUTHORS: What did this particular guy get out of this?

DANNY: Prestige in his job. Everyone patted him on the back and said what a great job he was doing.

AUTHORS: Did he ever use any of the credits for girls for himself?

DANNY: I don't know.

AUTHORS: How did these deals with the agencies work?

DANNY: A salesman would come to this particular fellow and say, "Hey, a client at such and such an agency is interested, do you know when he can make a visit?" The dispenser of the goodies would take care of it. He had a sort of weird bookkeeping system. For example, a salesman at this station was entitled to an override in goods when he was at his ceiling as far as income is concerned. In other words, if a salesman generated two million dollars in sales and that was half a million over his maximum quota, he didn't get paid the extra commission in cash. He got goodies. Simple as that. That's why at the end of a month all the salesmen would go to the goodies closet and pick out what they wanted. But it would depend on how many credits they had. He would have to deduct the credits from the salesmen's overall credits in the goodie closet. Example: You are the salesman. You have five points. Each point is a color TV. Let's say each point is five hundred dollars. You have twenty-five hundred dollars in points—goods. It's because the company has saved twenty-five hundred dollars in extra commission it would have to pay you.

AUTHORS: None of this gets recorded.

DANNY: No, this is tax free. If I got ten color TV sets as a result of this system, that's five thousand dollars in extra income that I don't report. So it works, as I was saying, like this. One of your customers has to be induced into making a sale, and he wants to get laid. So I say I'll take care of it, but I'll deduct it from your points in the goodie closet. When you come to me at the end of the month you have your credits or points, but I have taken care of one of your clients with a madam. Okay, that is deducted from your points. You are going to say that you drew fully from what you were entitled to from the goodie closet even though I have deducted one TV set. That set went to the madam who fixed up your client.

AUTHORS: Someone along the executive line has to know what is going on.

DANNY: Absolutely no. The sales manager knows. But that's as high as it goes. The general manager of this station was a very pristine fellow. All he knows is that sales are up, and that's all he wants to know.

AUTHORS: Everyone looks good.

DANNY: No matter how you slice it, if this ever got out and there was a scandal, the general manager would be out of a job. Simple as that.

AUTHORS: Did this operation exist before the guy who is now handling it?

DANNY: I would imagine that it did, but in a different way.

AUTHORS: Were these sexual services ever provided for people at the station?

DANNY: To my knowledge, they never were.

AUTHORS: What about you?

DANNY: I have three color TVs that didn't cost me a penny. I get a commission on the deal, absolutely. I was the connection between the guy and the madam. I was also the fellow who induced her to do it in trade. My deal was that no matter what she got, I got. Simple as that. One for one. And you say, how does he hide it? I'm telling you that with seventy thousand dollars' worth of goodies a month, he's got plenty of ways to hide it.

AUTHORS: Did anybody ever get an automobile?

DANNY: No. There'd be absolutely no way of hiding it.

AUTHORS: Mostly TVs and the like?

DANNY: This broadcasting outfit does fifteen thousand dollars a month with RCA on a trade-out. That's thirty TV sets at five hundred dollars retail. If you do it three months in a row, which is what the station has been doing, that's forty-five TV sets. There are ways to hide four, five, or six TVs.

AUTHORS: Does this go on at other radio stations?

DANNY: Absolutely. As far as I know, CBS does not do business in trade-outs except for restaurants so they can entertain clients and customers. NBC? Johnny Carson will go into the audience and hand out dinner for two at Luchows, for example.

AUTHORS: Does the madam you deal with take restaurant credits?

DANNY: Yes. Theater tickets, too. She's a cultured madam. I'm working out a deal now to recip [reciprocate or trade-out] some books. I'll be getting a sixty-dollar clock radio for arranging it. Nothing for nothing, buddy.

AUTHORS: Have you ever thought about blackmail?

DANNY: It's not my nature. All the people involved are nice people. They're doing what they have to do to survive. They feel it is a necessary part of what they do to make a living. Let me explain the situation with some of these people. Take the guy who runs the goodie closet, for example. He makes eighteen thousand dollars a year, which is nothing. He's upset. He figures he saved the company eighty-five thousand dollars in cash. Certainly, he figures, he should be worth one-fourth of that. He certainly should be making twenty-five thousand dollars, but he's not. He didn't get a Christmas bonus, didn't get a year-end profit-sharing deal. The salesmen? There isn't a guy there making more than thirty-seven thousand dollars except the sales manager who gets forty thousand dollars. I never heard of that sales manager having any direct dealings in this. But all the salesmen do. The madam has never been involved in a deal like this before, but she likes it. She operates seven girls full-time and has access to others.

AUTHORS: Have you ever thought of the possibilities of setting up arrangements like this at other places, in other businesses?

DANNY: Yeah. But it's pimping, very bluntly.

AUTHORS: You don't consider yourself a pimp?

DANNY: I do, and I don't. I consider myself what I want to consider myself. What other people think, I don't care. I don't consider myself a pimp because I'm not a manager of the flesh that is being traded. I'm negotiating terms, that's all.

The flesh trade associated with broadcasting is not limited to local stations such as the one described above. It goes on at the network level. At a recent dinner meeting at Sardi's in New York, the national program director of a network, in addition to picking up the dinner tab, offered to arrange sexual liaisons for each of the three-member affiliate advisory board dining with him. This same network maintained a suite of rooms in a nearby hotel for whatever entertaining it deemed necessary for the transaction of its broadcasting business. For a time the suite was the scene of a very high-stakes poker game. "It was available for other sports," quipped a young executive of the network.

Several years ago a New York radio station was known by broadcasting insiders as a station that hired girls for its staff because they would be available for sex.

Disc jockeys who used to take cash payola for getting records on the air find that they can still receive payments for plugging records. "What it comes down to is that the guys from the record distributors know that with certain DJs before a record gets a plug on the air, the DJ has to plug a broad," a record promoter confesses. The arrangement is usually made by the record promoter. "Out in the sticks, a DJ is satisfied with free records. In the big towns, and especially the ones where hit records are created, the DJs want more, and it's usually women they want," the record promoter explains. "When you deal with the really big names in the DJ business, the jocks often expect to get fixed up with the chicks who are on the records. A jock wants to screw the sexy young singer before he promotes her record on the air." Recently a young woman record promoter eliminated the use of girls by offering her own services to the love-starved stars of the disc-jockey world.

For a highly rated rock-and-roll disc jockey who carries a heavy clout with his record-buying audience, the pickings in the sexual groves are unlimited, whether it be pretty young girls from the rock groups, up-and-coming singers, or the flock of teenage followers who think every word from his lips is a heaven-sent pleasure. Hundreds of star-struck girls eagerly await the words, "Let's hop into the sack," from their favorite DJ.

A rock-and-roll disc jockey in a major city was notorious

in the broadcasting and record businesses as a fellow who liked boys. He was a top-rated DJ and consequently had his pick of the charming lads making up the dozens, even hundreds, of groups trying to get a hit record. The sharp record promoter aware of this DJ's sexual fancies usually showed up at the jock's office in the company of a handsome young man. "After the show, it was back to the jock's pad," the record promoter told the authors, "and within a day or two, the jock came through by playing the song I happened to be promoting that week."

While many radio stations try to avoid the possibility of payola by leaving the scheduling of music to persons not on the air, prices are still being paid to get a new release played and onto the popularity charts. In cities where a single play of a new record by one disc jockey with a tremendous audience—each member of which has money to spend on records—the denizens of the radio studio, the guys with the sure-fire chatter and glib tongue, make out very well.

Because broadcasting is centered in New York City, the location of the network headquarters, major agencies, and important brokers of time sales, the city is also the center for the payoffs that are so much a part of broadcasting in the United States in the 1970s. Deals are contracted on the basis of who is able to provide sexual services. More of this kind of dealing goes on than people in the broadcasting business care to admit. The sexual activity associated with broadcasting in Hollywood is limited largely to the production aspects of the business. "In Hollywood it's the old casting-couch routine," says an insider. "In New York it's the salesmen and time buyers and account execs who are the recipients of the goodies available in the flesh market."

On the question of the legality and the morality of broadcasting's prostitute payola, a high broadcasting executive stated, "This kind of thing goes on in all American industries. I don't think broadcasting can be singled out because of it, or should be."

The difference, however, is that broadcasting stations in the United States are licensed by the government to use public property—the airwaves—and are required by law to operate in the public interest. It would seem logical then that the Federal Communications Commission inquire into whether the public interest is served if the broadcasting business is conducted through schemes that involve illegalities, tax evasion, and trafficking in sex.

5

Bulls,

Bears, and Broads

"There is a certain irony in the fact that the intersection where the high finance of the world is centered is at Wall and *Broad* streets."

The executive who makes the comment sits in a high-back leather chair looking from a window in a skyscraper that towers over the financial district of New York City. A man in his fifties, the executive is one of those men in the financial world who cannot tell you his exact worth at any given moment. His holdings are so vast, his wealth so great that it fluctuates constantly. He began the accumulation of wealth in the great American tradition. "As a Wall Street messenger boy," he boasts with a twinkle in his eye. "There is very little about this financial jungle that I haven't seen, don't know, or haven't experienced," he says with a sweep of his arm to encompass the Wall Street towers below his window. "That includes the sex part," he adds with a thump of his hand on the rich red leather arm of his chair.

Sex is far from a stranger in the offices that line Wall and

Broad streets and surrounding avenues in lower Manhattan. The offices in the buildings lining the "canyon of heroes" where celebrities and heroes get ticker-tape parades as they ride up Broadway are the sexual playpens of the high and low of the world of finance.

"A man who is going to invest a lot of money in stocks on the basis of the advice of another person necessarily has to have a lot of faith in his adviser. The adviser, on the other hand, has to demonstrate not only his sound business judgments but a genuine personal interest in the man whose money he's investing. That means keeping in touch, going to lunch, being an all-round nice guy—a friend as well as an investment counselor," explains a Wall Streeter, and a very friendly guy. "Being a good friend means being a good provider."

One of the most successful providers "on the street" is Conrad, a rangy, sandy-haired young man only a few years out of Harvard Business School. Conrad earns a salary of six figures by being a nice guy as well as a shrewd business adviser.

CONRAD: I was never a naïve person, but I was initially surprised at the amount of pimping that goes on between investment counselors and their clients. I have one account who lives in Connecticut. He made a lot of money in his own business, but a few years ago he got out of actively controlling the company to devote himself to earning his living wholly in the stock market. That kind of guy is a big investor. It turned out that he was very dissatisfied with the brokerage house he had been dealing with. It was a very staid old outfit. I got a tip that this gentleman was unhappy, and a friend arranged for us to meet one day at lunch. The man was horny as hell, I was told by my friend, so I took along a young woman I knew who did call-girl work on the side. A real beauty. Well, this gentleman from Connecticut just couldn't keep his eyes off her. I made up this story about having made a date with this chick for that evening but was going to have to work late. I moaned about how she was going to be stuck. The guy's eyes lit up. He suggested that perhaps he might fill in for me. I played it cool and acted a little hesitant, but I finally said it would be okay with me if it was okay with the gal. She said it would be. What a pair of actors we were that day! So the date was arranged, but the clincher came as we were leaving the restaurant where we'd been having lunch. I whispered to the gentleman that this chick was a very hot lay and, if he wanted me to, I'd say something to her about being nice to him. I told him I'd tell her he was a very important client of mine. I figured he'd take the hint. If he didn't, I was going to be out the cost of lunch, the price of the hotel room where the chick was staying, and the hundred and fifty dollars I was paying her for taking part in this little plot. I was very edgy that evening and got very little sleep. Next day, I was really uptight, but a little before noon came a phone call from the gentleman to say how everything had worked out so well. I cooled it again, of course, and said I was very pleased to have seen everything turn out the way it did. He was very complimentary to me and said he was very grateful. Then I told him that I had had occasions in the past where I'd been able to do similar favors for other clients, and I was happy to do this one for him even though we weren't doing business. He said he'd like to get together with me and talk about possibly doing business. He wondered if I could bring along that same chick. I told him that was no problem at all.

AUTHORS: You landed his account?

CONRAD: After about three lays.

AUTHORS: You still provide women for him?

CONRAD: Oh, yes. The whole proposition is based on my getting him fixed up. If I ever stopped, he'd find some other guy who would line up chicks.

AUTHORS: It doesn't bother you being a pimp? You used the word yourself.

CONRAD: This is very big money we're talking about, and I don't see any reason why I shouldn't get my share. It's business. These men are going to invest their money anyway, and if providing women for them will get them to invest through me, I take home a very handsome living. I've got a wife and kids, house, car, the whole bit. It's business. That's all. Some guys, however, are too blind to see how they can use sex to boost their income.

Barney is a case in point. Young, bright, talented, and boasting top-of-the-class honors from one of the best business colleges on the East Coast, Barney worked for a major investment institution in New York. He managed a salary of close to $100,000 a year, due in large measure to an account based in Chicago. Barney provided everything a good investment counselor should—good information, good research, good advice. He phoned his client frequently. He forwarded valuable inside information. On the Chicagoan's frequent visits to New York City, Barney took him to lunch. Everything was fine, but suddenly the business from Chicago virtually disappeared. "I've given you good service. I've done a great deal for you, and I'm not getting your business anymore. What the hell's the matter?" Barney asked. The man from Chicago sipped his drink, set it down, and leveled his eyes at Barney. "I want to get laid," he said quietly. Now, at least once a month, Barney provides his Chicago client with a girl.

A Wall Street insider says the girls are top-notch. "No one on the street uses hookers as such. They are basically not hookers or call girls. They are models. Very attractive. This is accepted. Everyone does it."

A woman in finance bears a striking resemblance to Katharine Hepburn. She is often propositioned by her clients. "There was a particular fund manager who did business with a firm that I worked for. At a couple of cocktail parties he'd mention that I ought to be handling his account. I knew what he was really saying. Go to bed with him and get his account. I never did."

Many women in finance are not as attractive. A man in Wall Street noted, "Some of the saleswomen are not very attractive, although they are very bright. Either they're very wrapped up in what they are doing and they're too busy to pay much attention to themselves or they're overly tough, very aggressive, with no qualms about knifing the men they work with to get more business. And even if they were more attractive, it is very difficult for a client to say to a saleswoman that he wants her to make arrangements to get him laid. A client can say that to a man."

Wall Street women do use their sex, however. A young man who is the manager of mutual-fund money reports: "Let's say a fund manager with a great deal of money to spend is sleeping with a gal who is in the business on the street as a saleswoman or in the sales end of it. Let's say he's got a large order to place and has his choice of three or four people including the chick who's putting out for him. He'll give the business to her. This is how some girls play it."

"The girl who puts out can make more than a man in the same business with all other things equal," says an independent broker. "Let's say the girl works for a good firm, has good information, good research, and everything else that a man might have in going after the same client. The gal puts out, she'll get the business."

Women on Wall Street usually earn less than men, but the woman who uses sex as part of her business technique can do better than most men. A Wall Street source cites the following comparisons:

Salary (all other factors equal)

Salesman	$100,000 per year
Saleswoman	60,000 per year
Saleswoman who uses sex	150,000 per year

Availability of sex is not enough. The client must still feel that he is getting excellent service for his investments. Sex is what will make the client choose one firm over another when the firms are on equal footing in servicing the account. When prostitutes are used, the arrangement is identical to that in other businesses. The girls are high-class and cost an average of $100 per visit with a client. These costs are covered under entertainment allowances in the accounting departments and in tax returns.

So common is the pitch for sex to the woman in high finance that a woman can be unnecessarily on guard. One of them related an instance in which she was braced for a sexual proposition and prepared to deflect it. "I got a call from a very important client. He told me he didn't like going to lunch with the salesman assigned to him. He asked me to go to lunch with him. I thought I owed it to the company to find out what the problem was. Often there are personality conflicts between salesmen and clients. I went to lunch with the client, and I was expecting him to try to get me to sleep with him. It wasn't that at all. The reason he didn't like the salesman was that the salesman always talked business over lunch. This fellow just wanted a nice quiet lunch with no business transacted at all."

This same woman did have to deflect a pitch for sex from another client but at the same time realized that her boss had set her up in hope that she would take care of the client. "The three of us were at dinner and my boss just disappeared. He had specifically promised me he wouldn't just up and leave me with the client, but he did, anyway. In the cab when I reached my house, the client said he'd like to be invited up for coffee. I politely but firmly refused. He understood. There were no ill feelings. Next day, though, I let my boss know what a bastard I thought he was to pull a stunt like that."

The entertainment of important visitors from foreign countries is common among some Wall Street firms. "We will automatically have a party for these people, and we will see to it that girls are there, usually models," confesses a banker in charge of the foreign accounts for one of the biggest of the Wall Street banks.

Many women do business on Wall Street. Elderly women with huge financial holdings, important stock portfolios, and large sums to invest inhabit the milieu of the stock market. Widowed, with enormous inheritances, these grande dames dote on the attention of the countless young men who work in the canyons of the financial district. These men feel it is in their interest and in the cause of their companies to escort the wealthy ladies from Sutton Place and Beekman Place to fine restaurants, theaters, and the ballet or opera. "If being sexually attentive to a woman means I'll land an account that will put me in a six-figure bracket, well, I guess I'd do it," replied a young executive when asked if he would entertain the idea of sexually servicing an older woman.

Older men who delight in taking care of younger women find the intricate financial arrangements of the world of high finance make it easy. After the recent death of a mogul of the street, auditors turned up accounts for four women who were on the company payroll but not employees. They were mistresses of the late gentleman. He had been keeping them for years. They received salaries directly from the firm, and no one had ever questioned him or them about the arrangement.

"This business is basically very greedy," says a candid observer of Wall Street. "Any way they can get the business, they will do it. If a client wants to get laid every night by a different hooker, he can. There are hungry guys on Wall Street who will arrange it just to get his business. Wall Street is a whore's business. I guess all business is like that."

The executive in his high-back leather chair looking down on Wall Street nods knowingly when asked if he agrees that Wall Street is a whore's business. "The whole thing about Wall Street is how much money you can earn," he says with a smile. "That's the name of the game."

6

How Much Is a Bookkeeper Worth?

Standing over the corpse of Caesar, Mark Antony proclaimed, "The evil that men do lives after them, the good is oft' interred with their bones." That was before the Internal Revenue Service. Today, a man's good and evil is oft' interred in his books, but if evil is to look good, it takes a deft accountant. Sin on the expense account is the way of life of modern business. "Get your rocks off, sure," wisecracks a Chicago businessman, "but first get an accountant to write it off your taxes."

A man we call Harry Slater was in the gift-wrap business as a broker. Harry was a middleman between the numerous manufacturers of gift wrap and various concerns that used the commodity in their own ventures. A small man, balding, in his midforties, Harry Slater lived in Connecticut in a comfortable home, was happily married, and had three children. He inherited his father's business. Harry —who is now dead—is a typical story. The story comes from his tax man, George.

"Harry opened an apartment, which was also to be his

office, on the East Side of New York. He had a girl there who was truly a secretary. She got about a hundred and twenty-five dollars a week," George explained. The apartment was typical of East Side New York: large living room, which served as the office, kitchen, bathroom, and bedroom. "Two beds in the bedroom," George pointed out. "Now we're getting down to what he'd do. To wine and dine prospective buyers, he'd use girls, just as simple as that. He'd wine them, dine them, then let them use the apartment."

"Were there a lot of other offices in this building?" we asked.

"No. It was strictly a residential building. During the day it was his office. At night the office became a playpen. He used very high-class girls."

"He paid them personally?"

"The business paid. They were put on the books as sales agents. They'd get about one hundred dollars a night."

"The whole night?"

"Yeah, as far as I can see."

"How many girls did he use in a year?"

"About five or six."

"Would you say that he used them more than once a week?"

"No, it wasn't that frequent. Once was good enough to cultivate a customer."

"Did he do much traveling?"

"No," George replied, shaking his graying head. "Most people like to come to New York. You don't have to travel. They'll come here. It doesn't take much to get anyone to New York, especially guys from a small town. You get them to New York, and these guys are away from their families, and they're just as happy as pigs in a poke."

Harry's pattern was to take his clients to good restaurants—The Four Seasons, Johnny Johnston's—and spend a lot of money on them, knowing that the activities would be handled on the books by George. "Whatever he could get away with, he tried to do," George pointed out. "But the wheeling and dealing eventually got out of control until Harry's little brokering concern was broke. The strain got to him, and he died of a heart attack before the age of fifty. As his business went on the skids, so did his first marriage. Divorced and remarried, Harry left to his second wife the remains of the business, but before his death Harry worked for another man in a similar business, and for him Harry set up a call-girl operation similar to the one he had operated. But the second operation never reached the scale of the one Harry had going for himself."

In talking to the authors about Harry's way of doing business, George, the accountant, confessed his own naïveté at the beginning. "He'd use these names, these girls," George related with a grin, "and while working on the books I'd ask him what the hell was with these names? Then I put two and two together."

"Did he ever talk about the girls with you?" we asked.

"Very little. I know one of them got five thousand dollars."

"For an abortion?" we asked.

"No, she wanted to have the baby. She went to a place for unwed mothers. The baby was put up for adoption. That was when a lot of Harry's troubles started. Someone blew the whistle on him. Someone started giving him a bad name with all his suppliers, and that helped grease the skids before he went into bankruptcy. But Harry was never a guy to stay down long. He'd go up again. Things were on the way up when he died. He was a good businessman."

"Did he also screw himself to death?" we asked.

George gave a slow nod. "In a small way you could say he did."

Like others who use call girls in their businesses, Harry

expected a kickback from the girls—not in money but in sex. While the girls who put out for Harry and others like him could not write off their sexual activities in their own ledgers, these favors to the men who got them their business appointments, the kickbacks, were generally regarded as a standard part of the deal.

One of Harry's customers was unique. She was a woman, a buyer of specialty wrapping for a firm that dealt mostly in religious items—statuary, greeting cards, Bibles, and other objects of a sacred nature. A woman pushing 50, plump, grandmotherly, this customer was also interested in sex, and Harry did the trick for her until the woman laid her eyes on a handsome, muscular young man in his twenties who worked part-time for Harry. "You know, Harry," the woman said calmly one day, "I really would prefer that assistant of yours."

The young man blushingly confirmed that he kept the older woman contented. "But it was weird," he said with a chuckle. "Screwing that old dame at her pad with all those Christ pictures and Blessed Mary statues staring at us." The young man broke into laughter. "The first night I balled her she had this big plaster image of Jesus—the kind where the eyes sort of follow you around the room? I was banging away, and I kept feeling those eyes on me. Finally I stopped, got up, turned the picture to the wall, and then began again."

If Harry ever had any regrets or pangs of guilt about the way he did business, he never exhibited them. His accountant summed up Harry's philosophy: "What's wrong with it? No morality question at all. Hell, no. Everybody makes money. The girls get what they want, the clients get what they want, Harry gets what he wants. Who's getting hurt? If I can take you out to lunch or a ball game, that's legit. Why can't it be legit to get you whatever you want if you don't like a ball game? I'll get you something else on a Sunday afternoon."

Expense-account sex, veiled as it is under pseudonyms, doctored records, juggled ledgers, and padded vouchers, makes up a substantial amount of the "legitimate business expenses" deducted from income-tax payments by people doing business as individuals or as executives of corporations. A young producer for a television-network news department returning from a stint in Saigon wangled a cash advance from the Saigon bureau chief to cover his travel expenses home. The trip was to take him from Saigon to Rome, Paris, and London. On a four-hour layover between planes at the Bangkok, Thailand, airport, the young man sat at his table in the airport restaurant and drew up the expense account he would deliver to the network comptroller on his return. An expert at expense accounting, the producer concealed his planned sexual adventures in Rome, Paris, and London in his expense account before he had even reached those fabled cities. A lot of sin can masquerade as cab fares that go on expense-account reports without substantiation by receipts.

A man in the printing business has a staff of bookkeepers earning up to $400 a week each—far more than the average accountant, but these girls are far from average. Established in a midtown hotel, Edgar does all of his business through the use of these girls as prostitutes. Somewhat of a fashion plate, with an eye turned to the newest styles, Edgar has never gotten his hands smudged with printer's ink. He jobs everything out, acting the role of middleman between the client who needs a printing job and a printer to do the work. Edgar obtains business from his clients because he provides them with women.

With a long, thin cigar between his thin lips, Edgar adjusts his velvet tie and tells his story:

EDGAR: I rent these two rooms. This one is strictly the office. The other one is a kind of living room furnished with Castro-type couches. I've used a lot of girls over the years. They give me a competitive edge. A friend of mine was in here once when I was just getting the business started, and he wanted to know who the broad was. I said she was my accountant. He said he noticed that she never opened the ledgers and couldn't even type. That was true. But she was good in bed. She knew how to fuck, and it was her fucking that got me a lot of contracts. I have a large turnover in girls. Business depends on variety. Clients don't want to get fucked by the same gal all the time. So I change girls often. I don't know how many I've had working here. They make good money. A girl will see people in my office—three or four a day. Or she will go out to the client's office. I'll call and say that I'm sending my secretary over to pick up an order. That tells the client that he's going to get his rocks off when she arrives. I have no outside salesmen. I do my own selling. The girls help me do the selling. I like the idea of making money, and if it takes this sort of thing to do it, I'll do it. I *am* doing it.

An observer gets the impression that everybody is doing it, especially in the services industries where there is little difference between what one company has to offer in comparison with another. In printing, paper products, linens, and scores of other services, there is very little difference between one company and another except in the extras that a company can offer at the time it is seeking clients. As often as not, the extra is sex.

Ernie delivers sex along with sheets. He is in the commercial linen-supply service and runs a $500,000-a-year business. He says that 20 percent of his business is due entirely to his use of prostitutes.

ERNIE: About eighteen years ago there was a trade show, and I was talked into the idea of going into it by taking a booth in concert with another guy in the same business so the rates wouldn't be so exorbitant for each of us. We then asked ourselves how to stimulate business. We hired three girls and had an advertising man make up little outfits for them with our company names on them. The girls were hired ostensibly as models. Behind the booth we set up a little room, a bedroom. One cot. People were attracted to our booth because we were the only ones with girls—three beautiful blondes, girls about twenty-two or twenty-three years old. Naturally, the majority of the people who came over to our booth were men. They asked about the girls. Were they salesladies? I said they were, in a manner of speaking. When they asked what I meant, I told them that for a minimal order they would entertain. Where? I told them. But I made it clear that they signed the order blank first. In that little room in the back the girls would screw or fellate, but no one ever got into a girl until he came across with an order. Deliver or else no goodies. However, the idea of the show was not to get orders but to make customer contacts. The men from that show talked to their friends in the business and spread the word that by doing business with me they could also get into the sack with some nice chicks. That first booth cost a lot of bread—five thousand dollars. The girls were making one hundred dollars a day each. It paid off. Since then, the interest in being bribed with sex has jumped tremendously.

AUTHORS: Why is that?

ERNIE: All of these big concerns now have so many lucrative fringe benefits such as pensions, stock options, and so forth that employees have a vested interest in their companies and are afraid to take money as bribes or kickbacks for fear of being canned. So it came down to a very simple thing. "What can you do for me that won't show on the books?" There aren't many men around who won't accept a piece of ass. But then it gets complicated. Where does he get this piece of ass? You have to have a place—hotel, motel, apartment. You have a pad for it, and the girl is on your payroll. But there are dangers in this. A guy I know used a girl, a very smart girl. He used to send this gal out to close deals for him. She closed the deal with a good lay. She would put herself in bed for every order, but she was also keeping a little black book of her own, and came the day that she up and quit and set up shop on her own. She took that little black book and went to every customer in it and said, "Okay, buster, I have names, dates, and places. Either I'm going into business and I want your account or else people will hear that you have been fucking around on the side." She is still in business. She was bought out by a California outfit. Her share of it came to well over one and a half million. She's on a ten-year contract at fifty thousand dollars a year to stay with the business.

AUTHORS: How do you know that a client is interested in the girls you have to offer?

ERNIE: Once you meet a guy, you have a drink with him, or lunch, and you start talking. You find out how he plays it. If he lets you know he likes to play, fine.

AUTHORS: Where do you get the girls?

ERNIE: You have to use hookers. They're working a business, and they're working their business for your business. They're not going to get involved personally with the men they meet. They know it. They know they have to create the impression that they're in business for you. They keep it cordial but businesslike. Afterwards, they say, "It's been nice, but so long, Charley." You have to have more than one gal because these guys want variety.

AUTHORS: What would happen if you stopped doing this kind of business?

ERNIE: If I were to suddenly become a guy wearing a halo, a good fifteen to twenty percent of my business would drop off. These guys would say, "I don't need you." If I want that fifteen to twenty percent, and I sure as hell do, I can't stop. In the space of two years, I increased business by seventy-five percent. More than half again of what I was billing. If I was billing a hundred thousand dollars, two years after that, using girls, my business went up from one hundred seventy-five thousand dollars to almost two hundred thousand dollars. It was a remarkable jump.

AUTHORS: You've been in this business using girls for a long time. If you had it to do over again, would you operate the same way?

ERNIE: No. Over the years it has been a big hassle. Not everything has been peaches and cream. Every day a big part of my time is devoted to sex instead of to my business interests. Someone calls to thank me for getting him laid the night before. Another calls and says he's horny and wants me to get him laid. It becomes like Frankenstein. I said I wouldn't do it over again, but that was off the top of my head, maybe even what I think someone would expect me to say. But deep down inside I know I would do it all over again. I guess it has been fun, and I have to admit that I get a kick out of it when I fix a guy up and say, "Have a good time, Sam. When you're through, take the key and put it in the mailbox."

7
The Garment Industry

"The garment industry? What they do is they get buyers laid all the time."

The garment industry's action is in New York in the avenues around the big department stores—Macy's, Gimbels, Korvettes. Dozens of firms, large and small, inhabit lofts, floors, and entire buildings, and while the streets outside are jammed with trucks and Puerto Rican boys pushing clothing racks loaded with next season's fashions, upstairs in the offices the action is between the buyers of those next season's fashions, the girls who model them, and the manufacturers who serve as the pimps. "The layaway plan has become a prerequisite and standard aspect of most business deals today," observes one study of the garment business in New York. "Any organization that has a showroom hires showroom girls for the dual purpose of working and selling in the showroom, and many to help entertain customers intimately on the outside," the study noted.

A pair of denizens of the garment jungle, Phil and Sollie, talk about what's going on around the plain pipe racks:

PHIL: A friend of mine owns a company. It's in a building across from Macy's, off Sixth Avenue. There's a guy in the building called The Gunner. The Gunner gets his cookies off fixing up broads for guys in the building. He doesn't make a cent on it. We call him The Gunner because, you know, that's what you call a guy that shoots a lot in basketball. So, anyway, I call up The Gunner and say, "Gee, I'm lookin' to get laid." He says I have a choice. We can get a bunch of girls, or we can get a buffalo. I asked what's a buffalo. He says, "Well, she charges five dollars. A buffalo's on a nickel." So I go up to the office. All of these offices in the garment center have convertible couches. Castros. The buyers sit on it, and the broads lay on it. This beautiful doll comes up. Her name's Kathy. Lives in Jersey. We all get laid.

AUTHORS: How many of you were there?

PHIL: Four guys, but it's not a swing. In other words, three go outside.

SOLLIE: They wait, they take their turns. Nickel slot machine.

PHIL: But a nice broad. I drove her home. She lives in a good Jersey suburb in a garden apartment. Here's her story. She'll come into the city. The Gunner sets her up. She picks up thirty to fifty to seventy dollars a day. Then she goes back home. On the weekends she works as a manicurist in Jersey. Great girl, lovely kid. She was about thirty-one. She wasn't a hard hooker that you pick up on the street. She has a child.

AUTHORS: What about her husband?

PHIL: Dead. Vietnam.

AUTHORS: What else is happening in the garment industry?

PHIL: I get a call from another buddy. Same business. He says, "Phil, we haven't gotten together in a while." He was having a show at a hotel.

AUTHORS: A buyers show?

PHIL: Children's wear. All the buyers were coming in from out of town. This is a classic story. We stop in at the hotel, and we find out that if you want to get laid, you go to room so and so and see this guy in the business. So we go down there. It's the usual scene. All the Jews in the garment industry got to top each other. It's not how much you sell, it's how many broads you can get laid. You have to prove yourself to the other guys. That's the story in the garment industry. So, anyway, this fella has a secretary. He's paying her three hundred dollars a week, and she can barely type. But when the buyers come in . . .

SOLLIE: He turns her loose, and the buyers buy from him.

PHIL: It's a common thing. So this secretary takes my friend and me into the closet and blows both of us. Then her boss says, "You want to see something nice?" He gave us a phone number. Two days later we called up and mentioned his name, and then went up to Sixty-first and First.

SOLLIE: A beautiful three-bedroom apartment. Must have been going for eight hundred dollars a month.

PHIL: There are seven girls sitting in the living room. You make your pick, you go inside. It's like the old whorehouses. You go inside, you knock off your piece, you have a drink, and you move on. I took some good customers of mine up there. It's beautiful. You pick a girl; they are all beautiful girls. Another time, it was Yom Kippur night, but this was late afternoon and the place was empty. Just myself, my customer, and all the girls. Nobody else. Turns out that ninety-nine percent of their customers are from the garment industry. The girls call up some of the fellas who run the companies, and they get enough business from them and know that they're not getting schmucks off the street. They're getting businessmen. So this day we end up getting laid, playing cards, rapping, and it turns out that two girls own this operation. This girl Ruth and this girl Andrea. Ruth is in her midthirties. Andrea is in her early twenties. They split the profits. They were good for two grand a week just cutting in on the action. Ruth didn't go to bed with anybody 'cause she's going with a fella. Andrea liked to have a good hump around four o'clock because she woke up late. If you want it with her, yes, you had to pay for it. She enjoyed it. The other ones were hardened girls and new girls who just came in from out of town.

SOLLIE: Lots of college chicks get in on this, especially in the Easter season and during the summer. They come to New York sweet and nice, but in about six weeks they're hard as nails.

PHIL: They were picking up three to four hundred bucks a week.

SOLLIE: Earning their tuition money.

PHIL: I have a story about a college professor. Before he started teaching, he was in advertising. He used to have an office on Thirty-third Street just west of Madison Avenue, and his business was primarily in the garment center. He used to deal with people in the coats and dresses side. He did advertising for them. Many of these people used to need models, and he would get the names of young, good-looking college kids who were interested in being fashion models. He told them very plainly, "You want to become a fashion model, the surest way is to put your ass into the sack for me and for a photographer I know. He'll do a portfolio for you." I was there one day and he says to me, "Come up and spend a couple of hours, I want you to see how this thing works." During the course of about three hours I spent there, at least fourteen to fifteen kids walked in, and to each of them he said the same thing: "Look, you want to be a fashion model, you have to have pictures taken, you have to be photographed in the nude. You also have to lay down in bed. That's the way you get your portfolio." It became so . . . he didn't even give those girls a fair shake! He went into a room during the space of three hours with two of them because they appealed to him. He sent one to a photographer. He called him up as she was leaving and told the guy that this girl was coming over and that she was set up. He could take a few pictures and then give her a knock-off. She's ready because that's what she wants. So what does this photographer do? He spends half an hour taking about eight or ten shots, builds up a little bit of portfolio for the girl, and then screws her. That's how she pays him off. This deal between them got to be a regular factory. Out of fifteen in one day who came to see this guy, thirteen went along with the proposition. Two said they had to think about it. These are young girls, average age, eighteen to twenty-three—young, ripe, firm, good-looking. They all had good bodies because they wanted to be fashion models. These girls came in, and he came right to the point. "Honey, you want your pictures taken, you want me to do something, you've gotta fuck. If you don't, there ain't nothing going to be done for you."

SOLLIE: I don't know why they are so fucking desperate to get into this goddamned business. They must think there's glamour and money in it. They're ready to do anything for it. The garment center in New York is such that it gets everybody in there. They hear about these famous models making four hundred dollars an hour, and they want a piece of the action.

PHIL: Ninety percent of them are out of work most of the time.

SOLLIE: I know one gal, a fashion model, had two children, and she and her husband are divorced. She says that after being handled by every goddamned photographer and every agent, every one of whom was putting her into the sack, she was going to go out on her own. She came to me for help in getting a portfolio together. She said to me that she had no money to pay, but that I could have her in payment. Only trouble was, I had to go to her house, and when I saw those two kids running around . . . I said to myself, "The mother of these two kids has to run around peddling her ass to support them." I didn't have the guts to do it. I walked out.

PHIL: That was before you wised up.

SOLLIE: Today I take anything that walks. The lure of the garment center is such that these girls will do anything, and I mean anything, short of murder. They're opportunists. They find out that they can make money fucking. All they're looking for is the first opportunity to get out of where they are into something better.

PHIL: And they're ready to do anything for it.

Elaine

When Elaine saw an advertisement in a fashion magazine for a mink coat valued at $25,000, she made up her mind about two things: (1) to be a model like the one in the ad, and (2) to own a coat like that one. Elaine was 18 years old at the time. She is now 20. She has achieved both goals.

Elaine is not a naturally thin girl, but she has forced herself to follow a daily diet that keeps her on the dangerous side of being slender. She feels ill at times but never misses a day of work. Tall, slender enough to wear any designer clothes, and able to move with the studied grace of the accomplished model, Elaine regrets nothing of what she forces herself to do nor what she has done to reach the top in high-fashion modeling. In a candid moment over cocktails, she laughingly says, "I've spent as much time on my back as I have walking down a ramp at fashion shows."

Introduced to what was expected of her as a model through a racket similar to the one described earlier involving an opportunist garment manufacturer and a cooperative photographer, Elaine obtained her first portfolio by making love to both the manufacturer and the photographer. "The first was a thoroughly unpleasant affair with a man nearing sixty and with the manners of a pig," she recalls. "The photographer was really kind of groovy."

He was quite direct, she recalls as she reconstructs the scene.

"You understand what's involved with these pictures," the photographer said as she removed her coat to prepare for the photographic session. She replied with a nod. He nodded in return. "We'll get the shots out of the way first. Choose what you want from the wardrobe over there," he said with another nod toward a pipe rack crowded with high-fashion copies. They did evening gowns, cocktail suits, afternoon dresses, sportswear, and ended with a bikini.

"I must admit, you have a flair, baby," he said after the last shot. He stood close to her, his camera still slung on a strap around his neck. Gently, but insistently, he pushed down the tiny bottom of her bikini. She helped and when she was nude, he made a sweeping gesture, almost bowing, toward a couch. By the time she reached it, he had undressed. She expected him to pounce on her. Instead, he knelt by the couch and kissed her belly.

"Quite tender, he was, actually," Elaine concludes, brushing back the rich mane of lustrous brown hair that has made her world-famous. "And the portfolio was very nice. Quite professional. It got me some jobs."

The jobs at first were few. Between, Elaine held a secretarial job. She declined an opportunity to become a call girl. "It wasn't very noble on my part. I wasn't that desperate for money. Jobs, I was desperate for. My big break came with a TV commercial, but I had to turn a trick, is that the way to put it? For the producer."

He was in his late thirties with a wife and two children, but he was famous for a roving eye and a taste for variety in his personal life. As the casting director for a Madison Avenue ad agency, he had a wide variety of young women to choose from. He was drawn to Elaine by her hair, which was much on his mind because the commercial involved a shampoo product.

"I made quite a thing of using my hair to get him excited," Elaine laughs. "I just threw it over my face, and as I ran my tongue down his neck and chest and stomach, my hair followed like the vast and elegant train on a magnificent gown."

The shampoo commercial was an open door to other TV shots, and within two years Elaine had her mink coat, which she wears proudly.

Sara

Breaks have not been in the cards for Sara, an equally attractive girl who works as a model in the garment center itself. She has never been on a magazine cover, in a TV commercial, or on advertising billboards. She has been seen only by the buyers who come to the showings of the season's new offerings. Her figure is perfect for cocktail dresses not bikinis, but it is a good figure—round and full and comfortable. She is 23 years old and adds to her income by engaging in sexual acts for two firms in the garment center. "Sara gives the best head on Thirty-sixth Street," proclaims a man who makes it a point to hire Sara for his shows each year.

"Does it bother you having a reputation like that?" we asked her.

"No, why should it bother me?"

She says she believes that sex is an integral part of her profession. She regards it as no more extraordinary than modeling scanty undergarments or bikini bathing suits. "I make my living with my body, whether it's displaying it or using it sexually. There's no difference."

Despite the tough appearance and the defiant words, Sara appeared to be a young woman who was bothered deeply by what she was and by her failure to achieve what surely were her dreams of fame and fortune as a model.

Her career is far more typical of women in the garment industry than is the case of Elaine. Sara came to New York from a small town where she had been regarded as a very beautiful girl. A local merchant who had connections in the garment industry sent her to see some people whom he believed could help her toward a modeling career. She obtained a few jobs at which she learned quickly that more would be expected of her than looking stunning in a dress. When she resisted the propositions, the jobs became fewer, and she relented.

The assistant manager of a women's-wear firm introduced her to the specialty that was to win her the dubious title as the best fellatrix on Thirty-sixth Street. The introduction came during an interview for a modeling position. "You want this job, Sara?" he asked coldly. She replied that she did. He gestured to her to come over to his desk. "Go down on me and you have the job," he said, rubbing his hand into his lap. "I don't do that," she replied. With a shrug, the assistant manager announced, "Then you don't work."

After a moment's hesitation, she walked slowly around the desk, stared into the eyes of the man who still rubbed his hand into his lap, knelt before him, and waited with tear-filled eyes as he slowly opened his fly.

Telling the story today, Sara laughs. "He was disappointed, but he had to give me the job. I still see that creep sometimes on the street. I look right through him. This business is filled with germs like him."

Herbie

Herbie doesn't think of himself as a germ, although the girls he victimizes and uses have been known to describe him in even more vile terms. Herbie is a kind of agent. He sends garment firms girls both for legitimate modeling jobs and for prostitution. He insists he is not a pimp. "I'm what you would call a middleman," he says.

Small, wiry, and extremely nervous, Herbie darts about the garment district, dodging and weaving among the clothing racks and carts, dashing across the narrow streets from between parked and double-parked vans. He is always on the move. Even in his chair in his crowded, dingy office in the corner of a loft building, he is never still. He uses the telephone, and the way he uses it greatly resembles the style of the madam of a call-girl operation. Conversations are short, cryptic, and often blunt. "You want how many cunts, when?" he snaps. Or with a voice that is rightly defined as oily, he asks, "What's my cut of this here party you're having if I get you half a dozen chicks?"

Herbie proudly states that he pretests all the girls he sends out on assignments of a sexual nature. "I'm a muff diver," he brags. "I can turn a broad inside out with my technique. A girl wants to work through my agency, she's got to spread for me. Lots of times I don't even take a commission if the chick is really something special."

Herbie has been an agent of sorts for nearly 20 years.

Alfred

Twice a year, Alfred, a buyer of women's outerwear for a department store in Iowa, goes to New York City to look at the new line of garments. He always buys the lines offered by three garment firms. It is a ritual. He need not go to New York at all, and he would not (because he hates the city) except for the fact that twice a year Alfred is treated to visits to a house of prostitution where the women are choice. His routine with the women of the house is as predictable as the order for garments that he brings with him from Iowa.

The girl is blonde. Tall, with large breasts, she stands a few inches taller than Alfred, who is a small man with graying hair, Thomas Dewey mustache, and a softly slender physique. They drink Scotch, chat about the weather and the new women's coat fashions that he has seen that day, and how well he thinks they will be accepted in Iowa. Then he presses close to the girl and buries his face against her neck, nibbling lightly toward her shoulder. Fumbling with her dress, he manages with some difficulty to free one of her breasts. Rising to his feet, he asks the girl to stand and then slowly undresses her before he leads her to bed. Intercourse follows. He never removes his clothes.

"Alfred delivers business valued at one hundred thousand dollars a year to the firms who provide him with the willowy blondes he prefers to make love to with his clothes on," states a manager of one of the outerwear firms. "If we didn't fix him up with what he wants exactly, I'm sure that money would go somewhere else."

Helga

Born in Sweden, raised in America by distant relatives, schooled in Wisconsin, and in love with clothes and fashion since she was a teenager, Helga has the proud carriage of the Scandinavians. Her face is finely boned, delicate, and radiantly healthy. She never uses nor needs make-up. Her face is her specialty. As some fashion models are famous for their hands or legs or figures and are in great demand for photographic work emphasizing those areas of the female anatomy, Helga is wanted for her strikingly beautiful face. "It is a face that a man wants to kiss," says a photographer who works with her regularly. She earns an impressive income by turning that alluring face to the camera's lens, but in the early days after she arrived, a country girl from Wisconsin, Helga went the fleshy rounds in the garment district.

Her first fashion show has impressed itself into her memory.

The large, drafty loft had been decorated gaily with colorful walls of fabric. Colored spotlights added dramatic accents. Rows of chairs were arranged to form an aisle down which a low runway had been erected. This was covered with a golden carpet. Down this runway paraded the models with the full line of women's nightwear being offered by the firm sponsoring this showing. Helga, because of her proud carriage, modeled full-length, flowing, pink, sheer robes. Beneath them she wore only a bra and panties, but for the highlight of the show—the climax, the *pièce d'resistance*—she was to model an expensive and filmy nightgown without the bra and panties beneath. Striding down the golden runway, the garment flowing around her, her long, smooth legs were radiantly seductive in the soft lights that bathed the path she trod. Row upon row of buyers sat with jaws slack, mouths agape as she moved between them. Those closest saw clearly the dark circles of her nipples and the lavish growth of yellow hair at the bottom of her belly.

"We sold thousands of those nighties," she laughs, remembering.

After the showing, she was required to join the buyers and the sellers in the hospitality room arranged on another floor of the narrow, dingy building in the heart of the garment center. She coyly accepted the feverish compliments of the buyers, and when she was told by the owner of the firm that there was to be a smaller, more intimate party for some of the more important buyers in a suite at a hotel in the vicinity of Pennsylvania Station, she went along with six men and five other girls from the showing. "Helga," said the owner of the firm as he drew an elderly man toward her, "this is Ralph Roberts from Chicago. He buys for one of the biggest department stores in the Midwest. Be nice to him."

Helga liked the man and found his sense of humor incisive and self-deprecating in a charming way. He was gentle, even fatherly. He showed her pictures of his family. "My sons are in college. Nice boys. You'd like them, I'm sure." He laughed. "I *know* they would like you. They're chips off the old block, you know? They have eyes for pretty women."

"I felt a little uneasy," she recalls, "because it was like going to bed with my grandfather. He was a horny old gent. Three times we got into it. I heard that he placed a very, very large order with the company. He offered to get me one of those nighties for myself, but I told him that I got to keep the one I'd modeled. I think he was disappointed that he couldn't send me one. He said he'd send me something just as nice. And he did. A diamond pin. I still have it."

Lewis

Lewis arranges orgies for the buyers who come to town to see what his company is offering in its twice-yearly line of women's blouses. Dealing as he does with that item of apparel, Lewis chooses models with the physical endowments required to effectively display his wares. A pudgy, jolly man, he laughingly says, "I've always liked breasts. That's why I went into blouses. If I had been a leg man, I would have gone into stocking wholesaling; if I liked asses, panties." He shrugs, laughs so hard his big belly jiggles, and pushes an ever-present porkpie hat straight on his head.

A Lewis orgy is always in a private apartment rather than a hotel. Food and drink are catered. The orgy takes place in the living room, using several convertible couches. In one, a buyer from a Miami women's-wear chain stretches full length upon a nude model with his flushed face buried between the mounds of her breasts. Their hips work frantically. Just as rhythmically, the buyer lifts his face and gulps for air before resuming his lovemaking. On an opened convertible couch next to this couple, a gaunt, lanky buyer from California lies flat on his back while another buxom model straddles him. Their eyes are closed, their lips pursed. They are completely oblivious to what is going on around them. Another couple writhes on the floor. A fourth pair is a tangle of limbs and torsos upon a king-size Castro convertible. Over all hovers Lewis, order pad in hand and pen uncapped. He goes from couch to couch, taps each buyer lightly on the shoulder, and hands him the order blank to sign.

"You don't take part in these orgies yourself?" he was asked.

"Me?" he says, pushing the porkpie hat into place. "I'm a family man!"

8

How To Succeed in
Business by Procuring

In 1964, Joseph J. Ricciardi gave a party on his houseboat in Miami. The boat was notable for having been used as a location in the filming of the James Bond movie *Thunderball*. The luxurious houseboat suited Joseph Ricciardi's flamboyant personal style of living. He had a varied background as an operator of reducing salons, dance studios, charter-plane and boat services and had interests in real estate, stocks, and bonds. He dabbled in show business and public relations. At his 1964 party, he met Brigadier General Olbert F. Lassiter, president of Executive Jet Aviation. Three years later, Ricciardi went to work for Executive Jet Aviation, a subsidiary of the Penn Central Railroad, and began an association that was to end in the bankruptcy of the Penn Central, Ricciardi's dismissal from Executive Jet Aviation, a lawsuit by Ricciardi, and indictments against three top executives on charges of conspiring in their corporate activities to divert in excess of $21 million from the treasury of the Penn Central for themselves and others.

Charged in this celebrated case were David C. Bevan, the chairman of the Finance Committee for the Penn Central Railroad and its predecessor, the Pennsylvania Railroad, Charles J. Hodge, then chairman of the Executive Committee of DuPont-Glore Forgan and its predecessor company (investment bankers for Penn Central), and Brigadier General Lassiter. The indictment accused the men of diverting Penn Central money to Executive Jet, a business-jet operation that provided jet taxi service to executives on a subscription basis. "The steady flow of Penn Central money to Executive Jet was maintained by Lassiter's procuring of young women to accompany Bevan and Hodge on various junkets in the United States and Europe. These women were provided, in the words of one witness, to relieve 'the pressure that Bevan and Hodge were putting on Lassiter . . . because of poor monthly statements of EJA and Bevan and Hodge had to keep on pouring money from the Railroad every month into EJA to keep it going,'" charged the indictment.

Much of this testimony came from Ricciardi. It was given to Assistant District Attorney Carl B. Feldbaum and Lieutenant Israel Span in Miami on July 7, 1971, and to staff members of an investigating committee of the House of Representatives. To the House staff investigators, Ricciardi told of a meeting in New York City in the private pullman car of David Bevan on July 6, 1967, at which General Lassiter said Ricciardi could be of "great, great service to him" if he would help in the social life of General Hodge and Dave Bevan, since Lassiter was "under a lot of pressure from them due to the company having financial problems."

Ricciardi testified:

RICCIARDI: One one occasion, General Hodge asked if I knew of any young ladies who would go on a business trip to Europe he was taking with General Lassiter.

QUESTION: What did you do?
RICCIARDI: I found a young lady that I—was agreeable
to taking a European trip with an amiable group.
QUESTION: Do you remember her name?
RICCIARDI: Yes, Helene Avon.

In a statement given to authorities in New York City,
July 27, 1971, Helene Avon acknowledged the European
trip and corroborated Ricciardi's statement.

As part of his "public relations" duties, Ricciardi said he
provided girls on other occasions for the Penn Central
executives. In August 1967, Bevan, Hodge, and Lassiter
were planning a trip to Las Vegas and Los Angeles. Lassiter again allegedly asked Ricciardi to find girls. "One
was named Beth Greene—and she went with Hodge. David Bevan went with a girl named Corrine Grashal. General Lassiter took Michelle Newman, and I went by myself. I made the dates and ended up going alone,"
Ricciardi stated. Beth Greene backed up the Ricciardi
story with tales of their stays at The Sands in Las Vegas
and the Beverly Wilshire in Beverly Hills. Transportation
was by a new Jet Star plane belonging to EJA. Ground
transportation was by limousines at EJA expense.

"Then it would be fair to say these public-relations functions involved fixing up these particular individuals with
dates?" the House committee staff asked Ricciardi.

"As I said, General Lassiter said he was doing this himself, but he didn't have the time. He told me he had
gotten several dates for them in the past, but he was just
under such pressure with his own business and doing so
much that would I please assist him," Ricciardi replied.

Both officials of the railroad denied Ricciardi's charges
and dismissed them as "statements by a disgruntled employee."

Considerable procuring for purposes of sexual activity
is carried out under the banner of public relations by

personnel on the staffs of large and small companies or by the myriad public-relations firms that flourish in every city across the country. A recent study of the "sin-side of life" in New York City reported, "All large corporations have company panders or large lists of accessible girls for all purposes. This is standard procedure and done with discretion."

A young man employed by a large metropolitan broadcasting station provided extra services for executives of the station by arranging dates for the executives in a quiet, secluded, secure apartment maintained by the young man. His upward movement on the company organizational chart was regarded by those not in the know as one of the most remarkable success stories of recent years. Besides providing access to girls for station execs, this energetic young man also arranged for girls to be present at occasional station parties on such occasions as bachelor parties, birthday celebrations, or pot parties held by some of the younger station employees.

The personnel director of a New York communications outfit chooses carefully among the female applicants for secretarial jobs with the company to find those that his intuition and carefully phrased questions tell him will be accommodating to the officials whose offices he staffs. He does not regard what he does as procuring. To him it is simply "finding the right person for the right job."

In San Francisco, an elegant woman runs a model agency supplying people for photographers. She maintains two lists of customers—those who are interested only in photographing women and those who photograph them but expect to go to bed with them when the studio session is over. Another pair of lists includes the girls who do and those who don't. A subsidiary function of this agency is to provide models—men and women—for San Francisco's recently booming industry in hard-core pornographic films for theatrical showing.

The flesh trade remains in operation in Hollywood, although it has been in the doldrums along with the Hollywood film industry itself. Nonetheless, several agencies serve a lucrative clientele that is interested in attractive young people not only for films and TV but for the private parties that still occur in the posh homes in the Hollywood hills. At least one of these agencies sends scouts out to the sun-washed California beaches in search of "talent."

The aerospace industry is not immune. In Florida, California, Long Island, and Connecticut, where contractors and subcontractors are hard at work planning the hardware for journeys to the moon and beyond, there is a substantial trade in sexual favors. Bright young engineers have been attracted to one company rather than another because of the fringe benefits of easy access to beautiful women offered by one company and not another.

Similarly, defense-related industries find reason to use sex in the winning of important government contracts. High-ranking officers of all branches of the armed forces are treated to a wide variety of pleasantries in order to curry favor from them when they write reports about the prospects of a defense-industry plant coming across with the goods required by the contract. An evening a general spends in bed with a long-legged beauty often counts more in the winning of a fat government contract than all the specifications listed in the contract itself. When the contracts are not met and extensions are needed or additional funds (the infamous cost-override so prevalent in defense spending), the "favorable recommendation" forwarded by a Pentagon investigator may well have been garnered through a sexual favor. A highly placed official of a defense contractor told the authors, "I know of one instance involving a cost-override of several million dollars above the price of the item specified in the contract. A general looked into the matter, got laid at Las Vegas for three successive nights, and went back to his superiors with a recommendation that the contract be extended without penalty to the contractor. That general's piece of ass cost the taxpayers a couple of million."

The defense establishment that deals in billions of dollars each year is a ripe garden for anyone who wants to cultivate a share of those huge expenditures by providing women for men who can be influential when it comes to defense contracts.

The armed services themselves feel it is in their interest to treat important people kindly. Representative Henry S. Reuss (D., Wisc.) has charged that the U.S. Navy in 1970 entertained 226 civilians on cruises to such exotic ports of call as Hawaii, Bermuda, Puerto Rico, and Naples, Italy. Reuss charged that these junkets at taxpayers' expense cost $27,600 and brought the outlay in 1970 for the entire military complex to more than $600,000 in freebies for VIPs. Reuss got his figures from the government accounting office, which keeps the books on the defense department's "Joint Civilian Orientation Conference" and the "Distinguished Visitor Program" of the U.S. Air Force. Reuss was critical of these programs because he felt they amounted to propaganda for the military.

There was no indication from Reuss that these junkets included sexual favors to the VIPs, but long-time observers of the defense establishment maintain that such favors are easily gotten. "It's not an admiral or general, perhaps, who lines up the broads, but some junior officer down the line in the public-information office will usually have what the customer is looking for in the way of gals," comments a congressional aide.

Not all procuring of this nature is on the scale of that encountered in the Penn Central scandal or in other examples listed above. A young man interested in a career as a Broadway producer began his way up the show-business ladder as an assistant to one of the top names in the production of Broadway shows. The young man's job was to provide the producer with girls, but they had to be blonde, eighteen, and at least two inches shorter than the producer. When the producer headed for London or some other foreign capital, the young assistant was in charge of arranging for a passport and visas for whichever girl the producer happened to fancy at that time.

In almost every conceivable human organization the procurement of sex by one member of the organization for another is part of the operation. Soldiers in organized crime obtain women for their lieutenants. Followers of some religious cults recruit women followers for the potentates of the cults. Funds for the activities of some radical political groups are raised through the prostitution of women members of the groups. A source in the Federal Bureau of Investigation indicates that prostitution by women members of the Weathermen is common.

Some people have devised ways to obtain sexual favors for themselves while providing legitimate services for others. One of these opportunistic dealers in human flesh is Vivian La Stern, operator of an executive placement service on the East Coast. An attractive woman, divorced, and supporting one child, Vivian La Stern deals only in the highest type people. She places veteran executives, brilliant young engineers just out of college, and men leaving responsible government jobs for the higher pay and better opportunities in private business. She handles men only. Her method of operation is perfectly legitimate. Her ability to provide the right man for the right job is unquestioned, but part of her fee, if the male jobseeker suits her fancy, is an evening in bed with him. One of her most recent cases, she told the authors, was a handsome young man with impressive credentials as an electronics engineer. "However, the market for engineers—no matter how brilliant—has been in a slump," she explained. "But this guy was really terrific. I knew of one firm looking for just his type. Frankly, there were at least three other electronics engineers who could have filled the job. I got it for him. But not until we slept together."

As the young engineer waited, a little nervously, Vivian flipped through a file drawer. "I may have something. Let me check on it. Suppose you give me a call later today. No, better yet, suppose we meet for a drink and talk about it then?"

The young man readily agreed. Over drinks he agreed to dine with her. Over dinner, understanding at last what was required of him if he was to get the job, the young man agreed to accompany Vivian to her apartment. When he left her in the morning, he went directly to the office of his new employer and became one of the up-and-coming young engineers of that firm.

She guards against making an emotional commitment to the men she takes to her apartment, but she confesses that the young engineer struck a chord within her. "I've seen him several times since that first time," she relates. "It's not love or anything. He's just very pleasant. I remember thinking that he had the smoothest skin I had ever touched on a man. He had practically no hair on his chest at all. I ran my hands over his skin continually, stroking his shoulders and back and buttocks and thighs and belly. I guess we turned each other on because we went at it the whole night long with no sleep at all. The first time we were like animals in heat, all rush and no technique, but later we took our time and really enjoyed it. The thing about this young man is that for someone as brainy as he is and with a job that keeps him parked at a desk most of the day, he has a fine, athletic body. You expect sedentary people to have big asses, but his isn't. I guess he works out at a gym or plays handball or something. I never asked him. Maybe he just fucks a lot. That'll keep you trim."

She says she collects her special placement fee from only the choicest of the men who register with her placement firm. They are usually the young men. She likes young men, but she also feels that they are the ones who need the breaks to get started on good careers. She has never placed a man in a job who was unqualified. "He may be the best lover in the country, but if he hasn't got the qualifications for the job, I won't recommend him," she attests.

The routine has worked to the satisfaction of all concerned. Employers obtain the finest executive material available, able men secure excellent jobs, and Vivian has fun in addition to the fees she collects from the firms for whom she provides talent.

While some businessmen may not actually use employees as procurers, they do not hesitate to use the finances and the facilities of their firms to further their own sexual games. Stanley is a case in point. The vice-president of a supermarket chain, Stanley, with his boss Howard, has been a collaborator for years in an intricate system serving their desires while covering up their activities. Stanley was first introduced to sex in business before he rose to the vice-presidency. Then a buyer for his store chain, he had been in San Francisco for a meeting with Japanese fish-products wholesalers. "They made it a point to invite me up to their suite," he recalls. "They introduced me to a lovely girl, and I asked her if she wanted to go out to dinner. She said it wasn't necessary but that we could if I wanted to. Then I got the picture. I told my boss about it, and he seemed surprised that I'd been surprised."

Stanley's boss turned out to be a very surprising fellow. "When Howard was considering me for the vice-presidency, he had me checked out. A background check uncovered that I had been having an affair for a few years. Howard confronted me with the information but told me not to panic. He'd been playing around himself," Stanley reports.

Howard's affair was with his secretary.

Stanley laughs as he relates how no one in the firm has deduced what is going on between the president of the firm and his secretary. "Nobody ever connects them. Whenever he's away on a trip, she takes off, but everyone thinks she's just no good because she does that behind her boss's back. They don't realize that she's off because he's got her along with him on the trip. We've gone on several trips together. He'll tell me he's taking his secretary and suggests that I take someone along, too."

Careful duplicity is required of the arrangement that Stanley and Howard have made in using their business activities as a cover for their sexual play. Stanley says: "My family knows that three times a month I attend regional meetings in various parts of the country. However, I haven't been to one of those regional meetings in several months. We have very competent regional sales managers, but as far as my family knows, three times a month I'm away on business. I do actually go away, but it's not on company business. The two of us also find it easy to actually call company meetings in various parts of the country just to give us an excuse to get out of town. We have a meeting, but that's just part of the cover. In a way you feel you're cheating the stockholders, but we both have high-pressure jobs, and these little escapes help us to relax and perform better for the company."

The relationship between Stanley and Howard is very close and built on the mutual understanding that they are important to each other. They have devised a special way of handling bonuses paid to them from time to time. Part of the money goes directly to special bank accounts for use when they are on their various "business trips." The money is not reflected in their yearly tax returns but is listed as deferred payment.

The two men are aware that their underlings in their company are also inclined to have fun and games while on company business, but they regard this as a normal part of business American-style."We have a lot of buyers going to foreign countries," says Stanley, "and I understand they have some pretty wild parties abroad. They are prearranged, and I imagine the company is paying for them in some way. So long as the business keeps coming our way and the balance sheets are in our favor, I'm not going to ask questions. The same is true with our domestic operations. If our purchasing people are getting laid thanks to suppliers eager to do business with us and the quality of our own product does not suffer, I'm not going to go poking around."

Stanley is in the kind of business where sex is used to obtain business or simply for personal entertainment, but there are other businesses that are so competitive, so fierce in their vying for profits that sex becomes a tool to be used for the gathering of information. "Industrial espionage is as big as the CIA," quips a toy manufacturer. "In our business, when a guy takes a doll to bed with him, he'd better make sure she's not wired for sound. There are lots of modern Mata Haris in the toy business, believe me."

And not *only* the toy business.

9
Modern Mata Haris

"I guess it seems weird to you that somebody could be so excited about plastics," said an earnest young man with a shy laugh as he leaned back on a couch and put his arm around the girl sitting beside him in his apartment.

"Not at all," she said, leaning against him and pushing back a lock of brown hair that fell across the young man's forehead. "I find it very exciting to know someone who is genuinely enthusiastic about his work."

Outside a sharp northeast wind whipped snow from the roofs of buildings as the gusts cut across Cambridge, Massachusetts, toward the icy expanse of the Charles River and Boston on the distant shore. Snuggled together on the couch, the young man and the pretty girl stared at a fire crackling on the hearth. Presently she laid her head against his shoulder, and when his fingers tentatively touched her breast, she took his hand in hers and pressed it firmly against her. Her other hand dropped to his lap and stroked his thigh, inching upward until she grasped his erection. "A night like this should be spent under warm blankets," she sighed.

The young man stirred. "It is a cold night," he said, his voice cracking with a dry nervousness.

"Shall we go to bed?" the girl said with a smile that she pressed close to the young man's face.

"Yes," he moaned.

Brightly, she sat up and patted him on the shoulder. "You go turn down the bed, and I'll fix us some hot chocolate in the kitchen, okay?"

He laughed excitedly. "Okay."

From the couch she watched him go into the bedroom, then she rose and crossed his cozy room to a cluttered desk heaped with books, notebooks, sheaves of paper, and rolls of blueprints. She paused by the desk, scanned it with a discerning eye, and found what she was looking for. From her purse she withdrew a tiny camera. In an instant she had photographed four sheets of paper containing design specifications for a new plastic device to be used in a highly sophisticated refrigeration unit.

A foreign agent?

No.

She was an industrial espionage agent employed by a rival refrigeration company that needed the design of the plastic device, if the company were to remain competitive with the firm that employed the young man so excitedly turning down the covers of a bed he was about to share with the loveliest girl he had ever met—and certainly the boldest, frankest, and most accommodating girl in his experience.

By the time the bed was ready, hot chocolate steamed beside it on the night table. The young woman teasingly undressed while the smiling young man watched her from the bed. She had obtained all the information expected of her. Now, because she found this young man so disarmingly naïve and boyishly eager, she was prepared to give him the time of his life while enjoying the situation fully herself. Curling into her arms, sliding his feverish body against hers, the young man knew only that he was making love to a girl who spared no effort to make him happy. He never knew that the price for his orgasm was the loss of a competitive edge by the company that employed him.

Less fortunate was an executive of an electronics firm in Pennsylvania who began an affair with a woman he met in an elegant cocktail lounge in Philadelphia. She was all his wife was not—affectionate, seductive, and delightfully interested in sex for sex's sake. Meeting her once a week at her apartment, which was tucked away in a picturesque street near Independence Hall, the executive was impelled to tell the woman how much she had come to mean to him. In bed he talked softly and warmly about how much he enjoyed the things they did together. She responded to his need to talk by telling him she enjoyed hearing him describe how he felt and what he wanted to do with her. The language became coarser, the images more vivid.

Microphones concealed in the living room and bedroom picked up every word. Tape recorders kept them for future reference. Confronted with the tapes, the executive, rather than risk having the tapes sent to his wife, agreed to provide certain information about his company's plans for future development.

This man, too, had become ensnared in an intricate web of industrial espionage that never avoids the quickest avenue to a man's secrets—his sex life.

Industrial espionage, which uses sex as a tool, is an increasingly challenging dilemma in all aspects of American business.

In 1967 a report alleged to be the property of the General Motors Corporation stated that "within five years the gathering of intelligence as currently practiced by governments in both military and diplomatic affairs will become a formal, recognized activity of corporate management." GM denied that the report had come from its files. Whether the published report was legitimate or not, the gathering of corporate intelligence is a fact of life in American business. It is not yet "a formal, recognized activity," but it is most certainly an informally recognized one. Industrial and corporate espionage, like governmental espionage, has its Mata Haris, those seductive women who use their sexual appeal to purloin corporate secrets.

The 1967 report cited above notwithstanding, General Motors earned a reputation as a company that felt there was room in its activities for this kind of espionage. GM was found guilty of the practice in the celebrated case of Ralph Nader's.

The "consumer advocate" tangled with GM upon the publication of *Unsafe at Any Speed*, Nader's book about the safety hazards in the automotive industry, especially in the General Motors product the Corvair. Nader alleged that GM had hired private investigators to look into his private affairs, including his sexual life. GM officials admitted that Nader had been investigated, but they said it had been done without their knowledge. Nader filed suit against GM and collected. A Long Island detective, Vincent Gillen, testified that he had been hired by GM to investigate Nader and that GM officials had known about his activities. He said he had conducted more than 25 investigations for GM between 1959 and 1967 besides the one involving Nader. Others included in Gillen's probes were Danny Kaye, a Harlem antipoverty group that accused GM of racial discrimination, and officials of the United Auto Workers.

Industrial espionage is particularly acute in the auto industry where rivals seek to find out what styling and engineering changes are being made in competitors' products. *Time* magazine reported in August 1964: "Detroit's operatives keep in constant touch with key informants in such sensitive and hard-to-patrol areas as the tool and die shops, design firms, plaster shops, tire companies, and art studios that subcontract for the auto industry. Here they can often pick up information that skilled engineers and product planners can assemble into a faithful replica of a rival's new car."

Among the thousands of persons who work in these sensitive areas there will be some who can be reached through sexual enticements. A man who might not give away a secret for money might be coaxed into doing so for an evening of sexual intercourse with an attractive woman. Others might be easy prey for blackmailed information when caught in indiscreet moments of sexuality with a person or persons with whom they might not wish to be connected. Industrial espionage experts who use airplanes to photograph the test tracks of Detroit auto makers are cunning enough to know when to rely on the age-old allure of sex.

Sexual opportunists are at work throughout American business, not just the auto industry. In 1969 a Federal Grand Jury indicted a New York lawyer for allegedly supplying the "services of prostitutes" to an employee of the Securities and Exchange Commission. The lawyer was accused of conspiring to get information about SEC action for private profit. He owned stock in the Georgia Pacific Corporation, a paper company, and sought information on possible actions by the SEC regarding the company.

The toy industry, which is extremely competitive, is notorious for its use of call girls as espionage operatives. The young women are hired by various toy firms to seduce employees of competitors. Sophisticated recording devices are engaged to record the bedroom conversation as the women expertly lead their "clients" into discussions of their "work."

Arlene is one of these call girls, but she looks like the girl next door. Freckled, red-haired, and with a milk-fed, healthy sexiness, she has played the role of the girl next door on several occasions in order to obtain information for a major toy manufacturer. Once she simply moved into an apartment next to the target of her type of espionage.

ARLENE: The first time we used the girl-next-door bit was a few years ago. My employer learned that a competitor had just hired a really terrific designer of doll mechanisms. This man was an engineer, single, and making a good living. But he wasn't all that attractive. Glasses, you know? The studious type. We found out where the guy was renting an apartment, and we just rented one right next door. I became his neighbor.

AUTHORS: How did you get to meet him?

ARLENE: I'm all thumbs with things mechanical, so one Saturday afternoon when I knew he was home, I knocked on the door and asked to borrow a hammer. He loaned me one, but he also volunteered to hang the picture that I told him I was trying to put up. After that it was easy. I'd invite him over for breakfast on Sunday mornings. He was very flattered that I was interested in him.

AUTHORS: You seduced him.

ARLENE: Yes.

AUTHORS: His place or yours?

ARLENE: (Laughing) The bugs were in my place. I mean, hidden tape recorders, not real bugs. We had one in the living room with a mike concealed in a lamp by the couch. Another was in the kitchen under the table. A third was in the bedroom.

AUTHORS: Where did you hide that mike?

ARLENE: The headboard was one of those woven wicker affairs. Full of holes. We put it right behind that headboard. These are very tiny mikes. Everything in this business is miniaturized.

AUTHORS: How did you get him to talk about his work?

ARLENE: This guy was so turned on by me and his mind was so blown by the fact that I was interested in screwing him he just opened up. He got to be very much like a husband. The payoff came, though, when he forgot his briefcase one night. He'd been over for dinner, coming directly to my apartment without even stopping in his. In the briefcase were lots of drawings. I just whisked out my little Minolta miniature (camera) and snapped away. He was very broken-hearted when I moved out.

One of the strangest assignments undertaken by Arlene involved a professional football team's secrets that she obtained by getting to know one of the young men on the locker-room staff.

ARLENE: This kid had played football in college but never made the pros. Out of sheer frustration he got a job with a pro team and was little more than a glorified water-boy. But he did have access to secret plays.
AUTHORS: You obtained these for a rival team?
ARLENE: No, for some gamblers who put big money on the pro-football games.
AUTHORS: How did you go about getting the plays?
ARLENE: Well, as you probably know, the plays are in these little books that all the team members get. I just got the kid to bring home one of those books.
AUTHORS: You make that sound awfully easy.
ARLENE: I told the kid I was dying to learn all about football because that's what he was interested in. We'd sit in my apartment, or sometimes his, and he would go over the plays for me. It wasn't all that hard to get him to draw them on sheets of paper for me so I could study them at home. The hard part was that I actually had to study them so I would be able to talk about them the next time he came around. I got to be quite an expert on football.

Any industry that is engaged in seasonal competition has within its ranks individuals or companies that will do almost anything to learn what the competition is planning for the new season. Men in television programming find that the prospective program line-ups for coming seasons are extremely valuable items that competitors would like to obtain. A young man in the TV industry recounts an episode in which he discovered that he had been marked as a man who might spill some programming secrets. "I met a very nice girl in one of the East Side bars. It was one of those pickups you read about happening. She was alone, I was alone. I bought her a drink. We had dinner together. We went back to my place. I laid her. We had a few dates after that, and I started to like her a lot. She said she was in love with me. We talked about the future. She was interested in my job. When I asked her about hers, she said she was a typist with a firm downtown. Quite by accident, I discovered that she was working for another network. When I confronted her with what I knew, she went all to pieces and told me the truth. Fortunately I had not talked about anything that was really hush-hush. But that's what she was after. Too bad. Nice girl. Great lay."

Considerable internal "spying" occurs in high-pressure businesses. A news executive with a network engaged in an intense power struggle within the network induced his secretary to do some spying for him. "She used to go down on a guy in another department who had access to some things the news exec needed to know," reports another network official who was aware of the arrangement. "She didn't return with valuable information after every scene, but she came back with a lot of dope on what was going on. Her reward was to be included on the lists of people covering such news events as space shots and political conventions. She didn't go to Peking with the network's news team when Nixon went over there, but neither did her boss."

The stakes in industrial espionage are high. An editorial on the subject in the *New Republic* correctly pointed out that firms able "to devise the most effective means of using the new technology of business espionage will gain favored positions and higher profits. Their securities will rise in value and attract the interest of mutual funds, insurance companies, banks, and other depositories of the nation's savings and capital assets. Small attention will be paid to the means by which the gains are made. They will be institutionalized into the structure of profits and thereby pass beyond approach."

Corporations and government bureaus openly take a special interest in the sex lives of their employees, also. Part of their motivation is to avoid the possibility of an employee in a sensitive position being blackmailed. Homosexuals are special targets for this kind of probing, especially by government agencies. Homosexual rights groups argue that this is discrimination and are urging enactment of laws to prohibit discrimination against them in hiring. They state that if the government were not so discriminatory, the prospects for blackmail would evaporate. They point out that a person may be an admitted homosexual and therefore beyond the reach of blackmailers, yet still be banned from holding certain positions. "Blackmail has nothing to do with it, really," says a leader of the Gay Liberation Front. "It's just outright discrimination against gay people."

Corporate espionage frequently relies on the services of the private investigator. Even the largest companies will hire a private eye rather than use someone on the staff because they prefer to have as much distance as possible between themselves and their operatives. This is especially true since the GM-Nader affair in which memoranda and company files provided easy-to-use material for investigations into the episode. When reports are written, they are carefully handled and turned over to the most trusted employees at the highest possible level of the cor-porate-organization chart. In the GM-Nader case there was a "go-between" who acted as the connection be-tween a GM employee and the detective put on Nader's tail. Eileen Murphy, a former employee of the Justice Department, was named as the person at GM who dealt with the "go-between." In a letter purportedly written by Miss Murphy outlining instructions to detective Gillen, she allegedly wrote of her incredulity concerning reports of "what a great, charming intellectual this human being is—Eagle Scout type." Detectives familiar with the rou-tines of divorce investigations apply many of the same principles to the investigation of persons of interest to their employers. Tapped telephones, bugged rooms, per-sonal surveillance, photographs, motion pictures, and other clandestine eavesdropping techniques are used. The emphasis is directed to the subject's sex life.

"Sex is a common thing," reports a private investigator, "and a lot of people have these little quirks that they'd just as soon not have talked about. A guy may be cheating on his wife. Another might be keeping a gal on the side and using company money to pay for her. A fellow may like to fellate now and then. Maybe someone is into S and M. A case likes young girls, young boys, both. Who knows? That's the crucial thing. Who knows? To keep anybody from knowing a guy might be willing to go along with a proposition. Or he might feel that it's in his best interest to shut up about whatever he's been saying. In Nader's case, that guy was so clean it was unbelievable, almost unhuman. If you have nothing on a guy, there's no way you can shut him up. He just up and sued for invasion of privacy. Very few people are so clean in their private lives that they can file suit for invasion of privacy."

10

The Diplomatic Hooker

When it comes to sex, diplomats can claim no immunity. In some ways, the diplomatic representative is like the traveling salesman of the old jokes. He is on the road, away from home, often alone, and doing a selling job —except that what he is selling is his country and its foreign relations. But when the man in striped pants is far away from home, alone and lonely, he naturally turns his thoughts sooner or later to different kinds of foreign affairs. Every capital in the world has something to offer the diplomat looking for a good time, and in the greatest gathering of diplomats in the world—the United Nations —catering to the needs of these men is a big business.

Perhaps if the U.N. was located in the quiet of a small country and set among rolling hills and gentle valleys instead of being in the heart of swinging Manhattan, the personal needs of diplomats would be a serious morale problem for the world organization. As it is, the problem facing the U.N. is not that its diplomatic personnel engage in sexual escapades but that they be carried on without scandal and, hopefully, with no one noticing. New York City, with all its opportunity for anonymity, is ideal.

Prostitution thrives at the U.N., but the casual visitor to

the handsome world headquarters of the U.N. on the East River will be hard pressed to find obvious prostitutes at work. The girls who handle the U.N. are first-class women, elegant in their dress, worldly in their manner, sophisticated in their tastes, and discreet in their business. The chief of the Security and Safety Section of the U.N. issued a policy regarding the appearance of women on the premises. Ladies are expected to be "properly attired." The problem the chief of security faces is that anyone who a U.N. official wishes to take onto the property as a guest must be permitted entry. "If a delegate vouches for even a known revolutionary or prostitute, we have no authority to keep them out," says a security man.

If representatives at the U.N. want to be accompanied by prostitutes or to deal with them, it is something U.N. security can do nothing about. "There is no doubt in my mind with human nature as it is," says Chief of Security H.A. Trimble, "a certain amount of this thing goes on. I'd be surprised if it wasn't going on because a lot of delegates are here for extended periods on their own. Their wives and families are not with them. If they are not accompanied by their families, it would surprise me if they weren't taken care of one way or another."

They are taken care of by a flourishing coterie of girls who work the United Nations exclusively, mostly through madams who have established a working relationship with many of the more than 110 permanent missions to the United Nations. The activity takes place away from the U.N. premises, in the missions, in hotels, and in apartments throughout New York City. Many of these are in close proximity to the U.N. buildings, which are between Forty-second and Forty-ninth streets on Manhattan's East Side. Posh apartments in nearby Beekman Place, Sutton Place, and the East Thirties and Forties provide quiet, close-by retreats for the tired diplomat looking to shed the woes of the world along with his striped pants.

Despite the rules governing the propriety of persons admitted to the delegates' lounge, a diplomat can easily escort an elegant call girl into the lounge prior to an evening on the town and a night in the sack. It is an impressive beginning for a date. On the second floor of the Secretariat Building, the lounge looks out across the East River. In the distance a huge neon sign advertises Pepsi Cola, reminding the visitor that he is in the heart of swinging New York, the center for fun and games in the age of Aquarius and the Pepsi generation. Directly below the panoramic windows are beautiful gardens. The room is done in shades of brown and gold. Along one wall a row of telephones is available for important calls required of men conducting the diplomacy of the entire world. Colorful costumes from many lands adorn the men and women moving through this room. It is a quiet and comfortable place for a man to take the woman he'll be escorting that evening, even if she is a call girl.

Not far away are some of New York's finest European restaurants. A fast limousine ride across town is the Broadway theater district. It is a convenient, central location.

Into this setting walked Susan, a stunningly beautiful young woman in the employ of the Permanent Mission of the United Kingdom to the United Nations. Tall, statuesque, blonde, and elegant, Susan was typical of the kind of young woman who makes use of her devastating physical endowments to entertain at the United Nations. Employed ostensibly as an interpreter of several languages, Susan was in reality a call girl in the employ of Her Majesty's Government. Her story is told by a handsome, graying, sophisticated gentleman named Eric, who for years has been a denizen of the hazy world at the edges of international diplomatic circles.

ERIC: I first met Susan under very, very trying circumstances for her. She knew that I had certain sources with regards to, shall we say, people who could get girls out of certain difficulties. Her difficulty was very simple. She had met a man who had told her that if she would do certain things with him, he would give her all sorts of money. These were quite deviated things. Whippings were the least of it. Susan was naïve enough to accept a check, and every time she performed another deed for him, he added to the kitty. After nearly thirty-six hours with this man, the total was in the neighborhood of seventeen hundred dollars. The check, of course, was fraudulent. She got in touch with me, and I put her in touch with a person who could handle that sort of disreputable person. The character who gave her the bad time and the bad check was taken care of. Shortly after that Susan went to work for the British Mission. She was to be a hostess at parties and the like, and she was to gather whatever information she could. She was supposed to gather information about trade, boundary disputes, parliamentary sessions in various countries.

AUTHORS: How much money was Susan making at this?

ERIC: Her pay was two hundred dollars every two weeks from which she had to pay British and U.S. taxes. Her take-home pay was about sixty dollars a week. But the mission would provide her with free rent as long as she agreed to live in certain places. But after reporting verbally—never in writing—what she learned at the various parties she attended, she would find lying on her desk varying sums of money, anywhere from fifty to two hundred and fifty dollars.

AUTHORS: Was she also working on her own as a call girl?

ERIC: Yes. She never went for less than twenty-five dollars a trick and made as high as one hundred to one hundred and fifty dollars. She would average on her own between one and two hundred dollars a week this way. It turned out that at these parties at the U.N. she would meet some new John. Susan is a gorgeous woman, six feet tall in shoes, long legs, lovely blonde hair, and a fine body. She had been educated through all the British schools, married to a Frenchman when she was seventeen, educated by him in several languages, and then went out on her own again before coming to the United States. She never thought of herself as a whore. She always mantained some sort of dignity.

Dignity is the rule for sex in the world of diplomacy. Discretion is the by-word. The slightest breath of scandal could have serious repercussions. The diplomatic world still remembers vividly the Profumo affair of the 1960s in which a high-priced call girl was keeping the company of a British official and a Soviet officer. The scandal rocked the British Isles and brought down a government.

Prostitution in diplomacy is of two varieties. First, the kind in which Susan engaged, for the gathering of various kinds of information—espionage. Second, for the contentment, ease, and comfort of men away from home—sexual divertissement. The use of call girls for espionage purposes is done through the various embassies and legations as a regular part of their services to their home governments. Girls engaging in this activity are almost always listed as clerks, secretaries, typists, and other staff functionaries. The call girls used for nothing more sinister than sex are most often hired in the same way an American businessman hires them. There are several madams who maintain a list of girls especially for the diplomats.

"These must be really high-quality women," explains one of these madams. Providing dates for diplomats at the U.N., in Washington, D.C., and San Francisco, this madam requires young women with good educations, poise, and no aversions to race, color, or creed. "Many of the diplomats who come to this country from Africa or the Far East are interested in American girls," the madam explains. "I always ask the prospective girl if she would have any objections to taking a call from a nonwhite man."

The diplomat's madam will also be sure that her girls are willing to provide all the satisfactions that clients may expect.

"This is a world with an infinite variety of tastes," says the madam, "and in my business I have to be sure that those tastes are served."

One of the madam's girls, Veronica, has broad experience in dealing with foreign visitors. Also a tall, willowy, large-breasted blonde, Veronica has a regular clientele, one of whom is a general in the air force of a Middle Eastern country. He is a tall, sinewy man, dark-skinned, and over 60 years of age. He comes to the United States primarily as a purchasing agent for his government and conducts much of his business in New York. He has visited as often as four times a month, spending upward of $400 a visit on his date with Veronica in a quiet hotel in the East Thirties near the U.N. He usually rents a suite of rooms consisting of two bedrooms and a bath. The bath is essential, as Veronica explained:

VERONICA: The very first night I met him he brought me a whole box of pistachio nuts. They have pistachio nuts that are out of this world. They are about the size of a quarter. They dip them in lemon juice and lightly salt them, and you never in your life tasted anything as wild as those nuts. He was not in uniform and never is when I see him. He wears a regular business suit. He's always a perfect gentleman. He always brings me a gift. He tore my stockings once so he gave me fifty dollars to buy new ones. Once he gave me a bracelet.
AUTHORS: What happens with a customer like that? Is he any different from any other customer?
VERONICA: No. Basically a man with his clothes off is no different in any language. The only thing with foreign men is they try to ply you with liquor. They feel that they

have to get you drunk and that they are taking advantage of you. There's always foreplay. They never just jump on you. They talk a lot.

AUTHORS: What do they talk about?

VERONICA: They tell you how beautiful you are and why haven't they heard of me all their lives. The same old line. The general usually starts with, "I miss you, my darling, and it's been so long. I've thought about you in my travels." He always tells me I have beautiful toes. Then we head for the bathtub.

AUTHORS: The bathtub?

VERONICA: Yes. The general has this one little hang-up. He likes to fuck me in the ass in the bathtub. He fills the tub half full of water and then gets me in there. He's in back of me, and he soaps me and then he does it that way. He likes it.

AUTHORS: What does he do after that?

VERONICA: We take a shower. Then usually we sit and have a drink; then it's back to the bathtub for a second time. He always does it twice that way. He will never let me suck his cock, however. That's because he wants to kiss me, and if I do that, that's dirty. Then he takes me to bed and proceeds to make love to me. Would you believe that this general is sixty-two and is good for five or six times? Believe me! The very first night I met him I was with him from seven-thirty in the evening until four o'clock the next morning, and we went seven times. He says the reason he can do this is because he eats a lot of yogurt. He's very physically fit. Doesn't smoke. He does drink but not that much. He says drinking is bad for your sexual relationships.

AUTHORS: Aren't you afraid he'll have a heart attack?

VERONICA: Well, the last time I went to see him, I was starting to think about what might happen if this guy dropped dead on me.

AUTHORS: Does he talk while he's having sex with you?

VERONICA: Not much. He speaks at least seven languages, but when he's screwing me, all I hear is a lot of grunting and moaning. I guess that's the same in any language.

Another of Veronica's occasional clients was the governor of a small Caribbean island.

VERONICA: He was a very funny and entertaining man. He came up to me at a party one night and said, "Come on, I'm taking you out on the town. We'll paint the town red." We got as far as his bedroom. He tried to make love to me. He got on top of me, and I got him hard, but when he tried to lay me, he went soft. All the time he kept talking about his girl Lorita at home and how he was being a bad boy while he was away from her. Every time he talked about her he was no good with me.
AUTHORS: Was he married and Lorita was his girl friend?
VERONICA: Yes, exactly. What I could gather from the conversation was that his wife is an old matronly type. He's in his sixties. So he has this young girl, Lorita. He wanted me to be his New York girl, but frankly, I didn't think I could stand the competition.

Each of these meetings with visiting dignitaries had been arranged by a madam. "These diplomats and the like don't want to get caught," Veronica explains with a toss of her yellow hair. "They've got social position and prestige that they've got to maintain. They use someone whom they can trust to get them laid. They're all afraid of being robbed or blackmailed."

Keeping a proper public appearance is important, as Chief of U.N. Security Trimble pointed out in an anecdote about one of the delegates who came up to him to make a complaint. "This individual made the remark that there

that this type of thing could happen," said Trimble. "This organization is run by these delegates. It's their house."

Most of the diplomats at the U.N. are aware that the U.N. house on the East River is not a seemly place for them to pursue ladies that are available for a price; so much of the dealing in call girls by U.N. personnel goes on away from U.N. premises in the numerous missions throughout the city. But diplomats are active amorously in other U.S. cities—San Francisco, Boston, Philadelphia, and Washington, D.C.

Many of the embassies along Embassy Row in Washington, D.C., maintain open lines of communication with reliable persons who provide women. Rare is the Washington reception or gala party that is not visited by at least one diplomat with a beautiful woman on his arm—the woman being hired for the evening. Should any of these diplomatically credentialed men run into trouble, they know that every measure will be taken by state department officials and the Washington, D.C., police to see that there is no scandal. A scandal would be an embarrassment to everyone, so scandals are rarely allowed to surface.

The United States of America has diplomatic relations with more than 150 countries, most of which send representatives to Washington, D.C. These legations range from one-man operations to huge embassies employing hundreds of people. Those permanently assigned to an embassy will usually be accompanied by their families, but for transients and the single, a genuine logistical and morale problem is their sexual accommodation. As the nation's capital and centerpiece of the American democracy, Washington, D.C., is as accommodating as it should be. Again, most of the activity is through call girls working for known, trusted, and reliable madams. These operations also handle the American VIPs who live and work in Washington. Some maintain contacts in New York and

San Francisco in order to be able to make arrangements for dates for men who have to leave the capital from time to time.

The specter that hangs over all of these affairs is a sinister one—blackmail and espionage.

The most notorious incident in recent years involved the British minister of war, John Profumo, who was sharing the services of a call girl, Christine Keeler, with a Soviet deputy naval attaché, Captain Yevgeni Ivanov, in the early 1960s. While there is some question as to how much, if any, information was actually picked up by the Soviets in this affair, there is no question that the matter severely embarrassed the British. As Allen Dulles, the man who founded and headed the Central Intelligence Agency, observed, a Soviet intelligence officer "helped to undermine a government and its leaders. Thus he accomplished more to damage the Free World, whether by accident or design, than if he had obtained the intelligence information which he was apparently seeking."

Hanky-panky among the high and mighty of the international scene is not new. The Duke of Wellington was once asked by the Christine Keeler of his day—Harriette Wilson—to pay her for not publishing anything about him in her memoirs. Wellington replied, "Publish and be damned!" The men of the striped-pants brigade today are not likely to take such a courageous attitude. In spite of the fact that what concerns governments is the security aspects of a scandal and not the morality, men engaging in sexual hijinks while on the diplomatic circuit tend to be as sensitive to the possible moral embarrassment of any scandal as the security implications. In fact, the blackmail that may accompany an affair with a call girl will be based on the threat of public exposure of the diplomat's dalliances. His fear of a moral scandal is what makes him vulnerable to blackmail aimed at obtaining information.

In a television interview Allen Dulles was asked how

widespread was the use of sex as an espionage device. "I think it is worldwide," Dulles replied. "As long as there is sex, it is going to be used." He refused to answer the next question, whether the CIA employed sex as a bait to get information. He commented only to the effect that the United States recognizes "the existence of sex and the attraction of sex." The Russians earlier had accused Dulles's CIA of using sex to get at its Olympic team in Australia. "The American intelligence service," reported the *Literary Gazette* of the USSR, "did its utmost to force upon Soviet athletes an acquaintance with young women. Its agents more than insistently importuned them to 'have a good time.'"

Sex and sexual enticement are a part of the intelligence apparatus of all countries. It is especially true regarding homosexuality where the prospects of blackmail to avoid a scandal tend to be greater.

Short of an actual arrest for a crime, the diplomat working in Washington, D.C., need not worry about public disclosures of sexual escapades. Countless newsmen reporting the Washington scene and covering the state department are aware of what goes on behind the closed doors of Embassy Row, which diplomats are escorting call girls to parties, and who is providing what services for what people. The material goes unreported but not unnoticed. "Probably it's because we know these people on a day-to-day basis, see that they are human like the rest of us, and say 'fuck it, who cares?'" comments a long-time Washington newsman. With a grin, he adds, "Hell, if we started reporting the screwing that goes on in this town, it's all that we'd be reporting. Including the messing around that goes on among the press corps itself." When a scandal does break into the news, the judgment is never that so and so was a stupid ass to get involved in such an arrangement but that it was foolish of him to let it trap him.

A Washington call girl named Polly ("I chose that name in honor of the late Polly Adler," she explained) gave an insight into how her dates go:

POLLY: I get a call from my madam and she tells me to go to such-and-such hotel at such-and-such a room at a certain time. They are almost always very exclusive hotels, but not the ones downtown. The client is waiting, usually with drinks waiting, too. We'll have a few drinks. Sometimes we'll go out to dinner. More often it's sent up by room service. Sooner or later we go into the bedroom.
AUTHORS: Who pays you?
POLLY: I get the money directly, usually.
AUTHORS: Have you ever tried to get information from one of your clients?
POLLY: You mean spying?
AUTHORS: Yes.
POLLY: No. My business is screwing, not spying.
AUTHORS: Do you ever know who the man is? What country he represents?
POLLY: Sometimes. Sometimes I recognize the man. You know, from his picture in the papers or on TV.
AUTHORS: Did you ever wonder if you were in a bugged room?
POLLY: No. I figure these guys know where to go, where it's safe. Besides, it's not my problem if the room is bugged.

Quite the opposite of Polly is Joyce, a tiny, demure, red-haired girl who works the diplomatic trade in both Washington and New York. Her work in New York is usually handled by Eric, whereas in Washington she works directly for a foreign government through its embassy. Eric explains that Joyce was introduced to diplomatic work in New York on a modest scale when she was living with a low-level consulate clerk from a middle

One of the closest advisers to the president of the United States has a reputation as a ladies' man. One of his favorite pastimes when he is outside Washington is visiting bars that feature strippers and topless erotic dancers.

A New York City official gives a yearly Christmas party for a very select group of friends and associates. The food is fine, the drink is superb, and the girls are willing.

One of the most popular men on the college lecture circuit, in addition to his fat fee, requires his hosts to provide him with a selection of girls.

Baseball, football, and basketball players—professional sports stars—spend as much time in sexual sports as they do in the pursuit of the games that made them national figures.

The superstars of the rock-music world disport themselves with young girls who collect sexual experiences with the stars of the rock groups the way the bobby soxers of the 1940s collected autographs. Groupies are a fact of life in the music world of the 1970s.

Members of the Jet Set use their jets to get them from one bed to another and to orgies in the most exclusive spas in the world in a way of life that eclipses the sexual appetites of the Roman emperors.

"To be a celebrity today," says a veteran newsman who covers the doings of the famous, "means three things—fame, fortune, and lovemaking."

To be a celebrity is to have an open door to an unending celebration of sex.

Most of these celebrities fall into the category of "Beautiful People" as described by columnist Doris Lilly, who has been a close-up observer of them longer than almost anyone else. "No matter who they are, no matter where they go, there is one . . . major difference between the Beautiful People and the rest of us. They make love with less guilt. The poor man feels bad in the morning because he doesn't marry the girl. The rich man waits for the applause for his performance and is damned well put out if he doesn't get it. The poor man feels he has taken advantage of the girl and slinks from her apartment without a word, drenched in self-reproach. The rich man sees the experience as a two-way proposition. He liked it. She liked it. Let's get together soon. So long, honey," she wrote of the Jet Setters and their attitudes toward sex.

While not all public persons have such a callous attitude toward their sexual activities, many do. The attitude arises from a combination of money, arrogance, opportunity, and a sure knowledge that they will get away with it and with their public images intact as long as things don't go too far. Celebrities know that the journalists who bear much of the responsibility for making them celebrities will take care to see that their peccadillos go unreported. Newsmen depend on their news sources and will go to certain lengths to protect them.

The relationship of confidence between newsmen and the newsmakers is never more meaningful to both newsmen and newsmakers than in the world of politics and government. The human frailties, sins of the flesh, and private affairs of public persons go unreported, although not unnoticed. "Who is screwing whom gets talked about a lot in newsrooms but rarely gets into the news," confesses one of America's top political reporters.

Any gathering of newsmen who regularly cover political beats will feature stories about the doings of some of the most prominent political figures in a city, a state, or in Washington. Followers of Presidential Adviser Henry Kissinger have long swapped tales about Kissinger's legendary interest in and success with women. A newsman who covered Kissinger when Kissinger was on the staff of New York Governor Nelson A. Rockefeller recalls, "Whenever we got to town, whether it be Denver, New Orleans, or wherever, the first place Henry looked for was the topless joints, the strip joints, etc. This was his thing

Lobbyists, the people who are pushing for legislative enactment of certain measures, are aware of the proclivities of lawmakers and are not above holding out sexual favors as enticements for cooperation when it comes to voting. "One of the oldest ways to influence legislation is to wine and dine the lawmakers and provide them with girls," comments a political reporter. "Lobbyists usually have a bevy of girls that are available to somebody who may want the company of a girl."

Besides women provided by lobbyists or mistresses, the men who write the laws of city, state, and nation have other sources of women. Young girls attracted to a political figure or a cause are a source that is becoming more abundant as more and more young people are attracted to politics. Says another political reporter who has covered dozens of candidates: "They are attracted to the popularity, the charisma, of politicians. They start working in a campaign, on a staff, and some of them are so star-struck by this whole business that they are willing to be as accommodating as they need be for their candidate. You'll remember that the party on Chappaquiddick at which Senator Edward Kennedy had that tragic occurrence was a party given on behalf of some of the girls who had worked so hard for the campaign of the late Senator Robert Kennedy. These were young women drawn into politics by the personal magnetism of a candidate and also by the cause with which the candidate had aligned himself. Some young women today flock to young and handsome politicians the way they used to line up at the Paramount Theater to hear Frank Sinatra sing. It is the sex appeal of a candidate that draws many women volunteers into his campaign. Some candidates quickly learn that the devotion of these gals goes beyond politics to the bedroom."

At times a political figure feels it is in his interest to provide favors for the people who have worked for him or who may be helpful to him in the future. A newsman who covers the New York City government reports:

NEWSMAN: There is a certain city political figure who gives a Christmas party every year to which he invites a very select and very closed group of people. It's held in a restaurant out of the city, in a motel. He provides every party with an equal number of girls and invites male guests. There are rooms upstairs that he pays for, and whatever happens, happens. The girls he invites to these parties are specifically invited and know that they could, might, and will wind up in bed with the guests. This is a yearly affair that has been going on for a long time, and the people who are invited look forward to it. Every year they await their invitations.

It would seem likely that newsmen who are aware of such goings-on would partake of the activities, but newsmen interviewed for this book on the subject deny that reporters take part. One of them commented, "As a rule they don't get involved because the men who would be able to offer such enticements know that the reporter is likely to use the offer as the basis for a story. There is a very high degree of professional morality among newsmen, no matter what some people may think. Reporters may be as unpleasant and disreputable as possible as individuals, but when it comes to journalistic integrity, the overwhelming majority are straight, clean, and moral. They can't be bought with girls."

Another veteran of the news business agreed with those sentiments as he said with a fatalistic sigh, "The reporters I know who may be interested in sex while out on the campaign trail fend for themselves. It would be easy to ball some chick provided by the campaign staff, but it would compromise that newsman and everything he reports. We just don't do it. There's plenty of sex around college lecture circuit requires his hosts to provide him with girls in addition to his usual lecture fee. The deal for the girls is negotiated "up front" at the time the contract for his appearance is drawn up. In writing about the "Beautiful People" of the Jet Set, columnist Doris Lilly noted a German princess who recruited girls for her husband, an Italian industrialist who preferred whores to his wife because with them he need fear no deep entanglements. Another man keeps expensive designer dresses in his hideaway cabin to use as gifts for his girls, and other hangers-on in the world of the "Beautiful People" are either procured or procurers.

But no one attracts girls the way the stars of sports and show business attract them!

In his book *The Way It Is*, baseball star Curt Flood noted that baseball players use girls "medicinally, like an apple a day." Flood wrote*:

"If promiscuity is hit-and-run sex without emotional involvement, the baseball player wears the badge. At any given time during the baseball season, at least 366 major-league baseball players, managers, coaches and other glamorously uniformed types are away from home. Of these, at least 300 are randy as minks, a condition which becomes chronic in their earliest minor-league seasons, when they discover that no player need suffer sexual deprivation. In whatever stadiums baseball is played, and wherever the players sleep, eat, or socialize, avid women swarm."

Also testifying to the sexual goodies available to the baseball player was Jim Bouton in his book *Ball Four*.*

*From *The Way It Is* by Curt Flood with Richard Carter.
*From *Ball Four* by Jim Bouton, edited by Leonard Schecter.

"The great story in the bullpen tonight was about having this chick up in the room and she's saying, 'Tell me you like me, please tell me you like me, just tell me you like one thing about me, anything, just one thing you like about me.'

" 'Like you?' the guy says. 'I love you.'

"A pause. And the chick says, 'How can you love me? You don't even know me.'

"Which reminded another guy of the girl in spring training who was stood up by one player, we'll call him Joe, and went out with another instead. At the end of the evening, he finally coaxed her into bed, but not until after she said, 'I'm only doing this because I'm in love with Joe.'

"Which reminded yet another guy about something that happened to him. 'Right next to the ball park there was this little gas station,' the guy said, 'and after the ball game this chick and I parked there in the dark. We were at it hammer and tongs, I guess you could call it, when all of a sudden I see these lights in the rear-view mirror. Here comes this big electric utility truck and it pulls up side of us. The driver looks right in on us and says, "Nice game tonight. Go get 'em tomorrow." Jesus, I thought he was going to ask me for my autograph.' "

Sex is just as much a part of the pro-football player's training table as the baseball player's. Marty Domres of the San Diego Chargers, in his book *Bump and Run*, notes*: "One of the major fringe benefits of pro football is the willingness of young women to hop into the hay with even a lowly member of the kickoff team or the cab squad. It is not just the Joe Namaths and the other headline heroes who make out wherever they go—it is almost every player who wants to try."

Bump and Run, The Days and Nights of a Rookie Quarterback by Marty Domres and Robert Smith.

Television and its facility for creating superstars almost overnight has contributed to the phenomenon of freely available sex for almost any public personality. Faces are readily recognizable to millions of people. A loosening of the national moral code has contributed to the easy availability of sex, also. Today, a girl who might have been simply an autograph collector in past decades becomes a "body collector." This phenomenon is especially acute in the realm of rock music where very young girls—teeny boppers—deliberately set out to get their favorite rock stars into bed. These willing wenches soon were dubbed "groupies" because they chased after the rock groups that flourished throughout the sixties. Strong indeed was the rock star who could successfully turn down the advances of a young charmer who somehow found her way to his supposedly secret and well-guarded hotel room. The more opportunistic among the rock-group members deliberately chose the girls they wanted from the flock of "groupies" at the stage door.

More than a few show-business celebrities make use of the services of prostitutes. For many of the same reasons that a busy executive deals with call girls, show-business stars turn to them. Crowded schedules, unusual working hours, and the lack of time to pursue romances force some show-business personalities into the company of paid companions. Part of the advance planning for a star's arrival in a city will be the hiring of women and the scheduling of their meetings with the personality.

One of the top male singers has a reputation for using sex as a tranquilizer before his performances. A young girl is engaged to meet him in his dressing room before show time. She is hired specifically to fellate him. This often occurs with other people in the dressing room. Nude, the singer reclines on a couch while the hired girl goes about her work. No one acknowledges what is happening. She receives $200 for her services.

A film actor with a magnificent home in the Hollywood hills hires call girls regularly, some of whom travel with him to locations for films. When girls do not travel with him, his agent is expected to engage women for him in the cities he visits.

Yet another star—the object of adoration of numerous fan clubs among teenage girls—is known for choosing several of these starry-eyed girls from the flocks around his hotel, taking them to his rooms, and making love to three or four of them at a time. One of these girls said that she engaged in sexual acts with him and three other girls. "I guess there wasn't an inch of his beautiful body that wasn't kissed or caressed by one of us," she confesses with a girlish giggle. "He played around with all of us, fucking each of us in turn, but finishing with the one whom he liked the most. I was the lucky one. For a while I thought he was going to go all the way with this other girl, a friend of mine, but he left her and came over to me. A lot of girls settle for getting a star's autograph, but me? I had him inside me, coming, and that's much better than his autograph on a piece of paper!"

The private romances of public figures have always been a source of fascination for many Americans. Millions of fan magazines have been sold over the years because their covers advertise glimpses behind the scenes at the romantic lives of the famous, and although these magazines rarely presented what they advertised, the sales of the publications continued. In recent years one of the most popular personalities for the fan magazines has been Jacqueline Kennedy Onassis. A living symbol of the Jet Set, reigning queen of the Beautiful People, Mrs. Onassis finds herself always in the public eye. She has gone to court to maintain a certain amount of privacy and personal seclusion, but there is no sign that the public's curiosity about her is diminishing. A former steward on the yacht of Aristotle Onassis attracted considerable publicity when he revealed what he alleged to be the terms of the marriage contract between Mr. and Mrs. Onassis. The document according to Christian Kafarakis was so complex that it contained 170 clauses spelling out exactly how much money Mrs. Onassis was to receive each year and exactly how much time the two would spend together each year. The contract allegedly contained a clause stipulating "separate bedrooms."

Because the public remains intensely interested in the lives of the Kennedy family, the Kennedys bear a special burden that goes beyond that borne by other celebrities. Few people in American history have been so much in the public eye and subject to the public's curiosity as the Kennedys. Therefore, what might have been a routine tragic accident had it involved anyone other than a Kennedy became a national and international incident of supreme curiosity in July 1969 when a car driven by Senator Edward Kennedy went off a bridge on Chappaquiddick Island just offshore from Edgartown, Massachusetts, resulting in the death by drowning of Mary Jo Kopechne. Despite a formal inquest into the accident and a television appearance by Senator Kennedy explaining his actions in the tragedy, the incident at Chappaquiddick remained a question mark over Senator Kennedy and his possible future as a presidential candidate.

In the confines of the law, Senator Kennedy pleaded guilty to a complaint that he "did operate a certain motor vehicle upon a public way in said Edgartown and did go away after knowingly causing injury to Mary Jo Kopechne without stopping and making known his name, residence and the number of his motor vehicle." The judge at the inquest, James A. Boyle, concluded that "there is probably cause to believe that Edward M. Kennedy operated his motor vehicle negligently on a way or in a place to which the public have a right of access and that such operation

appears to have contributed to the death of Mary Jo Kopechne."

Mary Jo Kopechne's life ended in the cold, dark waters
of Chappaquiddick after an evening party given by Senator Kennedy for some of his aides and girls who had been
campaign workers. The group went to Edgartown, Mar-
tha's Vineyard, where Kennedy had raced his yacht in the
46th Edgartown Yacht Club Regatta. In the evening the
party went by ferry to Chappaquiddick Island for a cook-
out. There was good food and ample drink. Those attending were the senator, Joe Gargan (a cousin and close adviser to Senator Kennedy), other Kennedy associates
including Paul Markham, Ray LaRosa, Charles Tretter,
and John Crimmins (a chauffeur), and the girls who included Mary Jo Kopechne, Esther Newburgh, Maryellen
Lyons, Ann Lyons, Susan Tannenbaum, and Rosemary
Keogh.

Around midnight, according to Senator Kennedy, he
left the party with Mary Jo Kopechne to drive her to the
ferry slip so she could return to her motel. He stated that
because he was not familiar with the roads, he took a
wrong turn that led him to hazardous Dike Bridge and
that the car plunged into the water. He stated that he
tried unsuccessfully to reach Mary Jo and get her out of
the submerged Oldsmobile. He then returned to the cottage, he stated, and told Gargan and Markham what had
happened. The three returned to the scene for more un-
successful attempts to reach Mary Jo. Ten hours elapsed
before Senator Kennedy finally reported the incident to
authorities. Later, on television, he explained: "All kinds
of scrambled thoughts . . . went through my mind . . .
whether the girl might still be alive somewhere out of that
immediate area, whether some awful curse did hang over
all the Kennedys, whether there was some justifiable reason for me to doubt what had happened and to delay my

report, whether somehow the awful weight of this incredible incident might in some way pass from my shoulders."

The weight of the incident has not passed from his shoulders. Doubts remain about what really happened on the road to that fateful bridge. Judge Boyle himself expressed doubts about Kennedy's story. In his report on the inquest Judge Boyle inferred "that Kennedy did not intend to drive to the ferry slip and his turn into Dike Road was intentional." The testimony thus given by Kennedy at the inquest was, in the view of the judge, not the truth. In addition Judge Boyle said that he had found "inconsistencies and contradictions" in some of the testimony given by the 27 witnesses who appeared at the inquest. No criminal charges were filed against the senator.

The private lives of political leaders always come under close scrutiny during campaigns. For many years the fact that a politician was divorced was enough to disqualify him in the eyes of the American voters. Adlai Stevenson bore that burden heavily as he campaigned in 1952 and 1956, but a very public divorce by Nelson A. Rockefeller has had no noticeable effect upon his ability to be elected governor of New York.

Presidents lead private lives, but these matters are rarely brought out into public view while the president is serving in office or during the balance of his life after he leaves office. Only recently have historians written about the love affair between the late President Franklin D. Roosevelt and Lucy Rutherford.

The amorous activities of President Warren G. Harding remain closed to the public, however, because his love letters have been ordered sealed by the courts until well into the next century.

Members of the U.S. Senate have had a long-standing reputation as admirers of the female form. Much of this is little more than innocent flirting, as in the case of the late Senator Everett McKinley Dirksen, whose liking for the gals was always grist for the mills of writers and journalists. Annette Culler Penney, in her book *Dirksen: The Golden Voice of the Senate*, devotes a whole chapter to "Dirksen and the Damsels," noting*: "His office is deluged with letters from women wanting locks of his hair, asking favors of all sorts, sending him flowers or flower seeds or asking for seeds. Some have even asked him to make records for them. They swarm around him at parties and are not bashful about asking him for a kiss. One woman approached him at a reception and she told him she was a baby when he first campaigned and he did not kiss her then. 'So,' she said, 'how about making up for it now?' He happily obliged. He has often said that ladies are delighted to receive a kiss, and he felt it was a delight to kiss any charming lady. 'And,' he adds, 'they're all charming.' "

Members of the "most exclusive club in the world" and their next-door neighbors, the members of the U.S. House of Representatives, can be especially sensitive about the tinge of scandal. Congressional breaths were held in 1964 when it was revealed that a call-girl operation in nearby Maryland held in its files the names of 2,000 prominent men when the files were seized during a police raid. The *Washington Evening Star* reported that they contained the names of state and federal officials, a congressman, politicians, embassy personnel, professional athletes, judges, attorneys, sheriffs, newspapermen, and radio and TV personalities. The held breaths were released in a collective sigh of relief when no scandal enveloped the

Editor's Note: Dirksen did finally make some recordings, one of which became a bestseller. It was written and produced by one of the authors of this book, Mr. Jeffers.
*From *Dirksen, The Golden Voice of the Senate* by Annette Culler Penney.

pening. The better hotels will take steps to prevent open solicitation by hookers on their property, but what goes on in the rented rooms and suites is generally beyond their control.

"The most we can do as operators of a hotel system," says an executive of one of America's biggest hotel chains, "is warn our guests of some of the dangers involved in bringing prostitutes into the hotel. Our convention salesmen are instructed to give specific warnings to potential convention officials to caution their members about the very real dangers of robbery, muggings, and physical harm."

The dangers are not exaggerated. A Montreal businessman nearly died when a hooker he took to his hotel room while in New York City on business pulled a knife, robbed him, then stabbed him. Police told the man's wife that the stabbing occurred on the street rather than in a hotel room with a woman the man had hired.

Hookers who work the hotels of large cities often have other motives when approaching lonely men. They are scouts for partners in crime who later visit the rooms and loot them. Another system involves robbery of the John directly by the hooker's compatriot whom she admits to the room after she, herself, has entered it. Extortion is another game played by hookers and their associates who work the hotels.

All major hotels try valiantly to police their premises and keep them clear of prostitution, but they cannot prevent their guests from bringing persons into the hotel and to their rooms. This is especially true when a firm books a suite of rooms during a convention to use them as a hospitality suite. If girls are engaged to occupy the rooms as "hostesses," there is nothing the hotels can do.

A call girl named Lisa worked the convention trade on the East Coast. "In Atlantic City, I worked at the Traymore, the President, Haddon Hall, the Mayflower, and other hotels that I can't remember. In the daytime I'd walk the boardwalk. Guys would be out there between meetings, and they would set you up for the night. They would tell you what room, what hotel, and so forth. They would have parties going on at night, and they would have a room set aside. They called it the Playroom. That's where the sex was. I got anywhere from twenty-five to thirty-five dollars a 'pop.' Conventioneers on expense accounts tip like crazy, however."

Lisa says she was never bothered about hotel-security personnel. "I knew all the bus boys and the security men for the hotels. For a ten-dollar tip, they'd tell me what rooms were seeing some action. The bus boys used to set guys up with girls."

One of the more seamy aspects of Lisa's work in Atlantic City was having to deal with organized crime. "It's Mafia-controlled, and if you come in and you are not registered [with the police] and are spotted, the other girls will turn you in. A guy will approach you and tell you to have your man [pimp] get in touch. You have to get registered so the Mafia can get its cut of your money. You register with the police under the law, but the Mafia is in on it. The same is true for Florida. You register down in Florida with the mob."

Lisa knows quite a lot about organized crime and its connections with prostitution. "I was kept by somebody in the mob," she says, but she prefers not to talk in detail about the relationship she had with that top East Coast mobster. She fears for her life. "I don't want to be pushing up daisies in potter's field," she laughs. She knows from experience what can happen to the mobster's girl who goes awry of the rules of the mob. "My girl friend one time knew too much. She couldn't get away. They finally did do away with her, but it can never be proved."

Sex away from home for the businessman can also be organized. Recently, 85 people left on a trip to the Caribbean by way of a chartered aircraft. The chairman of the trip planned a raffle to be announced while the plane was en route. The stewardess aboard was enlisted in the fun to act as the announcer of the raffle. He told the girl that the prizes were (1) a bottle of Scotch, (2) a suitcase, and (3) "a surprise." About an hour into the flight the stewardess drew the winning raffles and announced the prizes, the Scotch to a pudgy couple, the suitcase to a balding businessman. Third prize, the surprise, went to a quiet, bespectacled man with a somewhat domineering wife. "What's the prize?" he asked, filled with enthusiasm. Down the aisle from the rear of the plane jogged a buxom young woman—a prostitute. "Here I am, honey," she giggled as she plopped herself into his lap. The winner, glancing at his wife, shouted, "What am I bid for this prize?" He sold her for $35. The young prostitute made much more than that in the hotel during the stay in the Caribbean by the travelers.

Sooner or later the traveling businessman faces the question, "How do I get a broad abroad?" Assuming that the traveler is not going to take advantage of various airlines' deals where the traveling husband can take his wife along on that business trip to Europe, the man heading overseas for the company, especially on a protracted journey, will have to contemplate seriously the prospects of finding some feminine companionship. If he is lucky, his hosts will handle the arrangements for him, but if not, he'll have to fend for himself. Prostitution in Europe is quite different from prostitution in the United States.

Bea, an expert on the institution of prostitution as it exists in Europe, is now living in the United States and earning a living in the mass-communications media. She was not a prostitute herself in Europe but spent most of her time in the cabarets and clubs as a legitimate performer where prostitutes were working. The following is a transcript of our interview with her regarding prostitution in Europe:

AUTHORS: If we were to ask you where to go in Europe for a good lay, what would you tell us?

BEA: Well, the first thing I would have to tell you is that you would have no trouble finding a girl. I'd have to ask you what kind of a girl you want. In Paris, if you were bisexual, I'd send you to The Crazy Horse. If you were straight, you'd go to any club in Europe. You'd have no problem at all.

AUTHORS: How much would it cost?

BEA: A lot of money. I'm not talking about what you'd give the girl. That's something you'd work out between you and her. But the minute you step into the club, it would cost you twenty dollars for a bottle. You slip the waiter a tip, have a girl brought to your table, and probably a bottle of champagne. If you stay for four hours—the average stay is three to four hours—count on spending a hundred and forty to a hundred and fifty dollars in the club. Not to mention what you give the young lady.

AUTHORS: How much of that does the girl get?

BEA: The last I heard it was about thirty percent.

AUTHORS: What is the average deal between the man and the girl?

BEA: About fifty dollars. It can be more. Depending on what you want to do. It also depends on the girl. There's a class structure among prostitutes.

AUTHORS: How does that work?

BEA: Well, you as an American would probably never see it because Americans are among the highest priorities with European girls. If you got a good-looking girl who was in the upper class of prostitutes and you could pay for it, she would go out with you. But she would very rarely

go out with a European unless she knew him well. These
are girls who have studied to be prostitutes. They've studied the ballet, they've studied art, they can talk on any
subject. They are used to living in wealth. They have
culturally acclimatized themselves to being the top of the
high-class prostitutes. They're not call girls as we know
them here. They work in cabarets as bar girls, and they
are some of the highest-paid prostitutes in Europe. They
work in the good clubs.

AUTHORS: Roughly how much do they make a year?

BEA: I think the German girls probably get the most
money. Germans and Swedes. Prostitution in Sweden is
not what it is in Germany. It's much more popular in
Germany. They would make eight hundred dollars a
week, just in money.

AUTHORS: There are outside gifts?

BEA: Gifts and hustles and everything else. Hustles refers
to all kinds of rackets where they can sell something.
Drugs, for instance. Gifts and hustles and everything
added to the eight hundred, a girl can make over a thousand a week. Let me explain to you the way prostitution
starts in Europe. I'll tell you about a girl named Chanel.
I met her in Germany. Her real name is Christina. She was
twenty-two years old when I knew her. She ran away from
home at age fourteen. Her mother had been a religious
fanatic. Christina ran away and took a course in beauty
culture, to become a beautician. She saw she wasn't going
to make any money at that, so she studied to become a
dancer, a ballerina. I presume she wasn't that dedicated,
but she was a good dancer. She went into striptease dancing on the side at night. She was very inventive. She had
worked out a whole routine on toe which she danced
nude—very graceful, very lovely girl. That's another
thing—most of the girls, most successful prostitutes if they
have any talent, are striptease artists. I say artists because

it is not a matter of taking off one's clothes. Striptease in Europe, girls dance totally nude with lighting effects and dancing. It's a real experience, quite lovely. The girls who work the bars really work, and I don't mean just on their backs. The European man is a very difficult animal, and you have to understand him and sympathize with him and play with him and hold his hand and listen to his troubles. In Germany many of these men are former Nazis and very brutal people. In France many of them are crooks and industrialists and Communists. It's hard work, and a European prostitute that just spreads her legs would have no success at all.

AUTHORS: What about pimps?

BEA: Pimping is less prevalent.

AUTHORS: You've known both American and European prostitutes. How would you compare them?

BEA: I find that black American prostitutes are very similar to the European prostitutes in their hard-nosed attitudes. They are out to make a living and hustle. Many black American prostitutes go to Europe and are very successful because they have something to sell, they have an art and an understanding of the man, and they are very cold-blooded.

AUTHORS: Does the black girl have a better opportunity at prostitution in Europe than here?

BEA: Naturally, because she's rare, she's in demand. There are very few African prostitutes. All the black prostitutes I met in Europe were Americans.

AUTHORS: You say you have a great respect for the European prostitutes.

BEA: Because they are highly intelligent people. When you sleep with a cabinet minister for a year, you become a diplomat. I mentioned Chanel—Christina. She's extremely aristocratic-looking and wore those big floppy hats. She was actually engaged to a count who didn't know she was a prostitute. She used to sleep with all these government people. Plus she'd turn tricks in the bar at night. She used to put all her money in furniture. She bought roomfuls, galleryfuls, storehousefuls full of antique furniture because she said that one day she was going to meet a man and marry him and wanted to bring something to the marriage. She saved her money. I'm sure she's got what she wants today, no questions asked. You have to respect that in a woman, especially in Europe.

AUTHORS: If you were surrounded by all these girls you admired, why didn't you become a prostitute?

BEA: I made better money doing what I did. Also, I wasn't hungry. I could afford to be moral about it.

AUTHORS: What would you tell a black American girl who would consider being a prostitute in Europe?

BEA: Don't go to Paris. I would suggest she go to wherever she had a friend to help her out, possibly Sweden, probably London. Prostitution in Europe is seasonal. The big prostitutes go south for the winter and come back in the spring. They go to Italy, Spain, Greece. American men don't seem to have much respect for the European prostitute, probably because they don't have much respect for prostitutes in this country.

It is probably true that the party girl, the hooker hired for pleasing conventioneers, or the call girl who takes care of the visiting fireman does not command much respect from the men she is hired to entertain. She is, after all, a living mannequin, a gal who pops out of a cake, a leggy and big-boobed broad who hands out drinks and canapés in the hospitality room. She is a body—not a person. She is hired for her body, not for her character or personality.

Yet personality is important to the successful call girl, and many of these women are among the most interesting, vivacious, and desirable women in the world. "The successful call girl is more than just a terrific-looking lay," says one of New York's most successful executive prostitutes. "She is a woman that men like to be with."

This young woman finds no difficulty in having the company of men who like to be with her. Her name is Platinum.

13
Platinum

In a desk drawer that he keeps locked and for which he alone has the key, the president of a major oil-products company keeps a little black book. In it he lists the names, addresses, and phone numbers of high-priced call girls. This executive sometimes uses these girls for his own pleasure, but mostly he calls on them to aid him in the conduct of his business, especially in entertaining important clients. His book contains more than 30 entries, but his favorite is listed under "P," for Platinum.

Platinum is one of the busiest young women servicing the top-echelon men of some of the most powerful corporations in America. Although she is perhaps more successful than others, Platinum is typical of the elegant call girls who are a factor in the conduct of business in the United States.

In many ways, she is a Horatio Alger story moved to the bedroom. Beginning life with neither inheritance nor social status and with only her natural talents, Platinum has climbed to the heights of success, and that is the essence of the American dream.

Platinum's business is almost entirely drawn from the ranks of business in New York City. Her clients have on occasion made up a substantial portion of the names listed on the roster of businessmen invited to dine at the White House in recent years. Some of those men have not hesitated to ask her advice on business matters, and she has not hesitated to give it. Some of her clients have actually taken her advice. One of them commented, "Platinum is a living example of business acumen. Why not take her advice if it sounds reasonable?"

Platinum is a happy whore. Her blue-gray eyes sparkle. She smiles a radiantly white smile and tosses the long golden hair that gives her her name. The money she makes keeps her smile radiant and the hair glowing. She lives in a fitting setting, conducting her business in a plush mid-Manhattan apartment, eating in the best restaurants, rubbing elbows with the Jet Set. She wouldn't have it any other way. She will tell you with a glint in her eye that a prostitute is a woman who does for a living what other women do for pleasure. And she will tell you that she takes her share of pleasure, too. "They say a hooker isn't supposed to have any kind of sexual feeling, but that's a lot of baloney. I'm a human being, I'm a woman, and if a guy stimulates me, I'm just like anybody else," she says with a wink.

While making feminine capital out of masculine interest has allowed Platinum a comfortable life, it wasn't always that way. It hasn't always been a bed of roses.

Nearly 30, Platinum has spent more than one-third of her life as a working prostitute. Before turning pro, she was a small-town teenager who gave it away. "From the age of fourteen I was messing around, screwing, blowing, whatever. I was pretty experienced at seventeen," she says with an honest, open face that hints of no regrets. It was at 17 that she decided it made more sense to sell it than give it away. "I was working. I had a legitimate job. I was sweating bullets for nothing in a factory job," she remembers. The pay

was $125 a week before taxes, often requiring a 12-hour
day. A coworker gave her the word about making extra
money by selling sex. The girl introduced Platinum to
some of her friends. "They turned out to be nice people,"
Platinum recalls, "and I was soon not only having fun, but
I was making money, too."

A marriage that went on the rocks made it possible for
Platinum to abandon the lean pickings of her native small
town and move to the big city—New York. Her husband
suggested that if she was going to be a hooker, she might
as well do it on a larger scale. He took her to New York
where she remained even though the marriage was a
failure. Her profession soon became an overwhelming
success. Now handsomely established in her plush pad,
Platinum deals mostly in men who have plenty of money
to spend on a woman, but she is not so far from her early
New York days on the street that she will forget an old
friend. She still has clients that pay her ten dollars, although her rate card is far above that level for her plush-
ier friends.

It is not possible to take a look at the life of the high-
priced call girl without a look at the streetwalker, the
chicks in the miniskirts, wigs, and spike heels who ply
their trade on the wild streets of the big cities. Most call
girls begin on the streets.

The life of a street prostitute has been described as "a
special world, a tough and lonely nether world—a society
with its own mores, its own social structure, its own style
of talking and dressing and playing, its own drug problem,
its own brands of violence, even its own snobbery." The
snobbery is evident in the street whores of New York.
"Oh, those New York girls," as the old folk song says. They
consider themselves "the smartest, best-dressed, most
glamorous, most desirable, most attractive, wittiest,
shrewdest, and sharpest hookers in the world." It depends
on which side of town they work. On the East Side plying

their wares along Lexington Avenue or around the posh hotels, strolling the edge of Central Park in the shadow of the stately Plaza hotel (technically on the West Side), the street girls are indeed flashy and glamorous. Draped in furs in the winter, sheathed in body-clinging minis in the summer, there is unquestionably a patina of glamour upon them. But their glamour does not diminish their brashness. "Hey, fella, want a date tonight?" they ask the solitary male sauntering up Lexington. "Want to go out tonight?" they ask the man heading home with briefcase swinging in his hand. Or eyeing the men in the bars stopping for a drink before going home to the wife and kids in the fashionable high-rise apartment house on the Upper East Side. At the end of her day's work, the East Side hooker is likely to go home to her own apartment in a similar luxury high-rise.

Not so the West Side street hookers.

Found along Seventh and Eighth Avenues, in the Times Square area, dotting the sidewalks around the midtown hotels, the girls are young, averaging in age between 18 and 23. These girls almost all work for pimps, many have drug needs, and doing business with them is, at best, risky, the risks running from being rolled to being found dead in a cheap hotel room, and in between those extremes, risking coming down with a venereal disease. The *New York Times*, in an article on the hard life of New York hookers, cited a West Side hooker named Dee as "one of those girls (who) . . . works Broadway from Forty-fourth to Fiftieth Street, begins work at two A.M., charges $20 for a ten-minute 'trick' and $50 for something 'special.' " Dee was described as 25 years old and a five-year veteran of the trade. The *Times* commented that she looked 30 and that, "ignoring the huge wig and the thick make-up, one can see that she must have been very pretty once—tall and statuesque, with smooth black skin and finely drawn features." The *Times* added poignantly, "But she is not so

pretty now, and it is not just the wig and the make-up.
There is a flat look in her eyes. Dee, like many of her
colleagues, seems totally devoid of emotion."

At first it may be emotion that sweeps a girl into prostitution, a need for love, for affection. Countless young
women follow the path taken by Platinum—young girl in
small town has a liking for sex, gives it away, learns that
she can sell it, sells it, then moves to the big city to sell it
at a higher price. One study of prostitutes in New York
City concluded that about 65 percent of them had come
from some other area of the country, most of them with
no intention of becoming hookers, but turning in that
direction when their dreams of success in the city failed
to materialize. "New York's atmosphere is very conducive
to the breeding, feeding, and general well-being of hookers," the study noted.

But for a native New Yorker turning to prostitution, the
New York atmosphere conducive to breeding hookers is
a sinister atmosphere—poverty and drugs. Many black
girls turn to prostitution to support drug habits, and it is
these young black girls who ply their trade on the West
Side and occasionally on the East.

In the class structuring of prostitution (between the
street girls and the call girls such as Platinum) is a wide
range of other girls turning tricks. There are part-timers,
college girls, nurses, airline stewardesses, housewives, all
looking for extra money. Dozens of young secretaries
were asked by the authors, "How would you like to triple
your income?" Their eyes widened, and they were eager
to listen. The vast majority continued to listen even after
it became clear that what we were talking about was
prostitution. We were merely interested in how many
would at least *listen* to the idea of becoming prostitutes.
Most did listen. How many may have actually followed up
the idea is a question.

At the top of the prostitution class structure is the call

girl. High-class, beautiful, cultured, these girls have their own private lists of customers, use no pimps, never work the streets, and charge a commensurate fee. Platinum is one of these.

Her upward progression from the street was a result of some disillusioning experiences. Coming to New York with her husband and turning tricks, she was moderately successful. She worked the midtown area, checking into the hotels on Seventh Avenue as a base, but her husband was often suspicious and brutal, and the marriage broke up. "I went on welfare and tried to go to school and get a start on a straight life," she remembers. "I went along for three months, but I just couldn't take it no more and started hooking again. Through a girl friend I went to work in a house. You build your own book and then you start to work for yourself."

Asked how many tricks she turned in one day during her stint in a house of prostitution, she smiled, pushed back her platinum hair, and said, "I saw forty guys in one day."

"Forty . . . guys . . . in . . . *one* . . . day?" we asked.

"I came out of there with two hundred dollars," she said wistfully.

"You must have had callouses," we remarked.

"You can't wear it out," she laughed. "It can go on indefinitely."

What Platinum got from her service in a house was not callouses but a growing list of clients, and when the list was ample enough, she set up shop on her own, working exclusively on the telephone from her own apartment. (The phone never stopped ringing during our interview.)

Platinum has left the streets behind her, presumably, although there are many aging women on the streets who were once high-class call girls. They aged, their clients sought younger beauties, and they hadn't put their money into the bank or stocks. These are the really tragic women. But Platinum, in addition to being a stunning beauty, is also smart, and her investments are right in line with her name—platinum. She will probably shift her interests from selling herself to running a house or a service with other girls working for her. However, she does not recommend prostitution to others. "You have to be tough. I don't mean hard, tough. You have to have a constitution that will take the pressure. Everyone thinks being a prostitute is glamorous. Let me tell you. It's not. You meet a lot of nice people, but of course you meet a lot of crazy people. There are a lot of perverts who come in under the pretense of seeing a girl normally and end up beating her or doing something violent or sadistic," she says.

"Are you happy?"

"Yes. I have a lot of fun."

"How much do you make a week?"

"A good week, three or four hundred dollars."

"That's good money."

"This business is not exactly the easiest job in the world. You have to be an actress. You have to be a wife, a mother, a daughter, and God knows what else. You have to generate a warm feeling for these guys."

The guys in her life are always a subject of fascination for Platinum. She thinks she performs a valuable service, saving marriages. "A married man that fools around is better off coming to a house with no strings attached. He pays his money and leaves. There's no love affair, no breaking up of a home."

Morality? Platinum does not regard what she does as being immoral. Nor do most other high-class prostitutes. Platinum, raised as a Roman Catholic, says she believes in God but doesn't believe in everything the church preaches. "God loves prostitutes just as He loves everyone else," she says.

The *Times* quoted another hooker with similar feelings.

"What's immoral is giving it away free, sleeping around with anyone."

The girls think their profession should be legal. So does the Reverend William Lewis, a Graymoor Friar attached to a midtown Manhattan church. Citing St. Thomas Aquinas, Father Lewis says, "Prostitution is a permanent evil and should be kept in a restricted place to protect those in other places."

The hookers have defenders among the ranks of Women's Liberation. A leader of the movement, Ti-Grace Atkinson, says, "My impression is that the prostitute is the only honest woman left in America. The suppression of women is synonymous with being forced into prostitution, but if that's the way it is, I say, let's not go for free, let's up the charge. Prostitutes are the only honest women because they charge for their services rather than submitting to a marriage contract which forces them to work for life without pay."

Platinum does not regard herself as the model of the new, independent woman. She regards herself as a working prostitute, leading a life-style she herself has chosen and which has given her a comfortable ride so far.

The life-style of the high-priced, high-class, elegant call girl is as high-class, elegant, and high-priced as she is. They live in the best neighborhoods in expensive and posh apartments. In New York it's the Upper East Side. In Boston it's the exclusive new apartments overlooking the Charles River or in new town houses in Back Bay. Chicago call girls look out from apartments on the lake front, from high-rises along Michigan Boulevard and Lake Shore Drive. Philadelphia girls have equally impressive addresses, all of them within easy reach of downtown and the corporate towers from which so many of them draw their clientele. Rents run in the neighborhood of $300 a month—for some girls only a part of a week's earnings.

Wardrobes are costly. The girls who date the boys from

the executive suite have to be ready to step into the finest hotels and restaurants and blend into the setting. Taste is required, and taste runs into money. So does the weekly laundry. A sizeable portion of the call girl's clothing budget goes for articles that only her clients see—underwear, lingerie, special nightgowns, and sleepwear. Jewelry is an added expense.

Trips to the beautician and the cosmetics counters count for another major share of the call girl's expenses.

Many call girls pay a handsome fee each year to tax experts who find ways of writing off expenses and shaving the amounts that the working girl pays to federal, state, and local tax collectors.

Another expense that call girls often encounter is the payment of protection money. A recent investigation of police corruption in New York City spotlighted a payoff racket connected with prostitution. A Madame X, identified as Xaviera Hollander, a call-house madam from the Netherlands, said she paid police $18,000 for protection. Her comments came after public hearings by the Knapp Commission focused on her call-girl operation and attempts by some policemen to collect protection money. Money was to be paid for tips from the police of possible raids or other harassment. A patrolman and an undercover man for the Knapp Commission were recorded on tapes on which the two talked about how the protection system would work:

PATROLMAN: What we'll do . . . we'll set up some kind of code. Like if somebody should call and say, "This is Mr. White from Chicago." (Whistles) Boom. Shut down. That's it. . . .
UNDERCOVER MAN: Hmmm.
PATROLMAN: "Mr. White from Chicago will be up at four o'clock." That means, man, knock it off until you hear from me. Lay off it a day or two.

UNDERCOVER MAN: Yeah, well, then let's do it that way. Let's just use what you said. "Mr. White from Chicago."

PATROLMAN: Mr. Black from Chicago.

UNDERCOVER MAN: Mr. White. Let's make it Mr. White.

PATROLMAN: Mr. White.

UNDERCOVER MAN: She doesn't like blacks. (Laughs)

Madame X claimed that she never got the protection she paid for. "I don't mind paying protection," she complained to newsmen, "but I should get value for money."

Jealousy is another factor that the call girl must deal with. A frustrated customer, a miffed colleague, a disgruntled madam can be the cause for grief. One very successful call girl was arrested because a jilted boy friend blew the whistle on her.

DETECTIVE: We got an anonymous complaint from someone who obviously knew this woman very well. It was a guy jealous of her. I kept my eye on her apartment for a while. One day I saw a guy leaving. I approached the fellow and told him who I was. As soon as I did, he panicked. He said, "Please don't tie me in with that apartment." It was funny. He said he had a sick wife and didn't want any scandal. All I wanted was verification of what was going on in that place. He said it was true, prostitution. He gave me the phone number and a name to use. I went up. The apartment wasn't that great. I made an arrest.

Still, with all the hazards and uncertainties, the call-girl profession flourishes. The allure of easy money for sexual favors is great. A young woman told that she can double, triple, or quadruple her income often finds the proposition an enticing one. Virtually all of those who decide to become prostitutes do so willingly, knowing in advance what they are getting into. Those who remain say they like the work.

"I make in one night what most girls make in a week, pay little if any taxes, have a nice apartment, plenty of clothes, get to go on exciting vacations, and meet interesting and exciting men," a girl says happily. "Why should I give this up?"

Former call girl Barbara Hart, who testified before a legislative hearing on prostitution in New York, says call girls have a good life and can earn as much as $100,000 a year. "The amount of clients a prostitute has these days has declined over the past, but still there are a certain number of men who will only be able to receive total satisfaction by paying for the sexual favors in cold cash. Sexual liberation has tended to take away from the prostitute's business, but still, a man who gets involved with a girl on a free basis is risking emotional involvement which may tend to mess up a family life that he has and is satisfied with. A call girl by the fact that she accepts cash relinquishes her emotional rights. Intimacy breeds emotional dependency. A girl doesn't like to be taken advantage of. She likes to get something in return. For a married man, this can be very difficult. He may be able to take her out to dinner or a show, but he may not be able to pay her rent or lavish her with gifts. In the case of a prostitute and her client, this kind of situation never arises. For a certain amount of money at the call-girl level he gets warmth and affection."

Barbara Hart gave up prostitution because she got married. She has no regrets about her former life. "I've rid myself of all my sexual inhibitions. I certainly have a much groovier attitude."

Never arrested and never considering what she did immoral, Barbara Hart felt that she was being very humanitarian because she was helping men overcome probis that she couldn't have operated on a much larger scale. "A space-age Polly Adler," she laughed. She wouldn't say how much she earned in her career. "I don't want the government after me."

The working day starts late and runs late. Most girls begin the day's business in mid- or late afternoon and keep going until the wee hours of the morning. One girl interviewed for this book described one day's work. "It began with a very nice gentleman, a vice-president of a firm on Madison Avenue, at four-thirty in the afternoon. He came to my apartment and stayed about an hour. He left in time to catch his usual train to Darien. Half an hour later I had drinks at the Plaza with another executive, this one with an insurance outfit from out of town. He comes to the city a couple of times a month and stays at the Plaza. After him, I had late dinner with another regular. I'm not sure what he does for a living. He looks like a Mafia type. After dinner we went to my place. He left around two A.M. I'd about had it for the day and was going to bed, but the phone rang. A party. Another girl was calling and could I come over to such-and-such an address. I went. Got home at eight in the morning."

This girl's "billings" for that day:

Vice-president:	$ 50.00
Insurance executive	$100.00
Mafia-type:	$200.00
Party:	$100.00
Total	$450.00

Because prostitution is an illegal activity, there is no official record of the income brackets of girls like the one described above. Estimates range from $30,000 to $100,000 a year.

The fact is, the average elegant call girl can take home

The fact is, the average elegant call girl can take home a minimum of $500 a week. The emphasis is on *minimum*. Many earn much more, and if you add the extras—the gifts from appreciative and extravagant customers—the income for the elegant hooker is considerable.

In their off-hours, call girls are about the same as other working girls. They go to the movies, watch TV, read, take vacations, shop, and even date. One recent study of call girls found there was "very little" evidence of a strong interest in gambling, perhaps because the "gambling urge" is so much a part of their daily lives. In a way, every time a girl agrees to do business with a new customer she is gambling on his trustworthiness. However, much of the entertainment that a call girl enjoys—theater, concerts, and dining in expensive restaurants—comes from the client, and in her off-hours she is most likely to do the things that she would not do with one of her Johns.

What a girl does with a John is, according to most girls interviewed, to make the client feel like a man. "They want to be men and prove it to themselves and to me," one girl told an interviewer. She admitted she would do anything the man wanted in order to satisfy him. "What he cares about is having a thrill with a girl and being a man with her," she stated.

Platinum agrees with that sentiment, and she does whatever she can or must do to please her clients—always with a certain sympathy for the obvious fact that the client cannot get what he wants and needs at home.

Often that is nothing more bizarre or complex than simple affection. Like the Japanese businessman who finds that a visit to a geisha for the sympathetic ear of a lovely woman is a necessity, the American businessman finds that a call girl can be far more sympathetic to what he has to say than is his wife who, likely as not, will simply heap upon him more woes and troubles. The call girl for the harried businessman is someone who centers her whole attention on him and his needs, who gives herself wholly to his desires, and who pampers him for the brief period of time he remains with her. There is no nagging, no discussion of family finances, nothing to keep him from relaxing totally.

Other men find that call girls perform sexual acts for them that their wives will not. Often, the men need considerable help from the girls to be able to perform. "If a man is having trouble," says a call girl, "I'll do almost anything to help him. If this means acting out his particular fancy, fine. Why not?" Why not, indeed? But many of the men who use the services of call girls do so because their wives at home can usually present a long list of reasons why not.

Insecurity is a part of the clients who see girls like Platinum. Outwardly they do not appear insecure at all. They are successful men with thriving businesses, good families, impeccable social standing. But they have deep-seated doubts about themselves as men and find that by performing well with call girls they can allay their insecurities. "I think the more class a girl has, the more men will look on her as a symbol of their success," reported one call girl. "A man respects you if he pays you a hundred dollars. He goes away boasting that he just screwed a hundred-dollar call girl. It's a status thing."

Platinum agrees with other call girls who suggest that a major role of the expensive whore is to work as much on a man's ego as she does on his penis. "You've got to reassure them not only of their sexual prowess but of their roles as successful men," she says.

Some of Platinum's clients would hardly seem to need reassurance. One of her clients is the head of a multimillion-dollar steamship company. An elderly man, he has a particular "scene" that Platinum plays out for him at every session.

14
Tricks of the Trade

The American male doing business with a whore is as much of an American tradition as ma's apple pie and the Fourth of July. For decades the encounter between the American male and the paid woman has been a source for literature, drama, and films. Holden Caulfield in *The Catcher in the Rye* as he fumbles and blushes through a liaison is the very essence of the attitude of the American male toward prostitution. He knows about it, is interested, gets up the courage to see one, and then is overwhelmed by his own embarrassment and insecurities until he finally blurts out, "Look, I don't feel very much like myself tonight. I've had a rough night. Honest to God. I'll pay you and all, but do you mind very much if we don't do it?"* This is literature's genuine portrait of the American male—not Tom Sawyer, Huck Finn, or Hemingway.

Kinsey noted that the percentage of males frequenting prostitutes in 1953 was almost precisely the same as 20 or more years earlier. There is no evidence to indicate any change in the figures over the past 20 years.

The Catcher in the Rye by J.D. Salinger.

Prostitution shows no signs of becoming an anachronistic profession. If anything, it is on the increase. There may be some evidence to indicate that there is a decline in the use of prostitutes by young men because of the changes in sexual morality evident in the young today, but it is evident that most of the clients of prostitutes through the years have been older businessmen, not the young. Surveys for this study of the sexual activities of the men and women in the executive suite indicate that the overwhelming majority of those men using call girls are older men. "The young guys today are getting it for free," stated a call girl interviewed. Then with a wink and smile she added, "Or they think they're getting it for free. In the end it may be the most expensive lay they ever had, because they may end up married."

There are several reasons why businessmen turn to call girls:

1. Boredom with their marriages; the male menopause.
2. Business purposes.
3. For many celebrities and busy public men who travel a great deal, the call girl provides quick sex.
4. Need for fulfillment of special sexual appetites.
5. Psychological problems that permit them to perform sexually only with prostitutes.

The reasons businessmen use prostitutes are as varied as the men themselves, and it is dangerous to generalize, but for the prostitute, the men are generalized—they want sex, they are willing to pay for it. The girls call them Johns. If it were possible to present a composite picture of the average John (and it isn't safely possible), he would be:

Age: middle thirties and older
Financial status: above average
Education: high school or better
Marital status: married for several years with children

The incidence of use of prostitutes rises sharply in a period that some psychologists call the male menopause. "It happens to a man in his middle 30s through middle 40s," writes David Maxwell in *Man and His Health* in *True* magazine. "He's happily married, or at least he's reasonably content with his marriage. His kids are growing up with no more than a normal number of problems. He's content with his job and its future prospects. He seems to have life licked. And then—*boom!* It all blows up. Suddenly he's pursuing Another Woman or maybe a whole bunch of Other Women."

Dr. Roger Bernhardt, a psychologist, adds, "The kickoff is the feeling and knowledge of one's own aging. At a certain age which differs from man to man, this can result in a kind of panic. That's when the trouble starts."

The specter of impotence arises, and the man seeks reassurance that he is the same lusty fellow he used to be.

The prostitute is one way of proving his prowess.

Johns fall into several categories:

1. The Friendly John
2. The Voyeur
3. The Busy Man
4. The Harried Husband
5. The Specialist

The Friendly John. This man is as much interested in finding friendship and companionship as he is in having a partner in bed. He is interested in dating the girl, taking her to dinner, to a show, to drinks afterward, and then to bed. He is likely to call just for conversation. He is often generous and is likely to be lavish with gifts.

The Voyeur.   This man likes to watch sexual activity and may masturbate while doing so, or when he has watched whatever scene he has paid for, he may join in intercourse himself. The voyeur will often prefer to observe two girls performing sexually together. Another type of voyeur is the John who likes to have one girl watch while he performs.

The Busy Man.   On the road, on the move, and too busy to spend a lot of time on the make, this John hires a girl to give him sexual satisfaction. Intercourse is always included in his itinerary.

The Harried Husband.   Frustrated and miserable at home or just plain bored, this married John gets from a call girl what he can't get at home. It may be a special sexual taste—oral love, analism, or other fetish that his wife refuses to perform.

The Specialist.   These Johns have very unique tastes in sexuality ranging from masochism to sadism to no physical contact whatsoever. Men who would find it difficult to find willing partners pay for them.

Of eight Johns interviewed for this study, the categories listed above were evident, as shown in the accompanying chart:

"JOHNS"

	Age	Occupation	Income	No. of years seeing call girls	Mar-riages	College	Type
A	45	Executive	$ 25,000	8	1	Yes	3
B	36	Junior Executive	15,000	2	0	Yes	2
C	52	Retailer	20,000	15	1	No	4
D	38	Teacher	14,000	8	0	Yes	1
E	40	Teacher	12,500	15	1	Yes	5*
F	39	Laborer	9,500	5	1	No	5†
G	47	Executive	23,000	10	2	Yes	3
H	55	Corporation President	75,000 plus expenses and stock.	20	2	No	3

* Prefers anal sex and use of rubber equipment such as dildoes.
† Sadistic tendencies.

John A:

Typical of the successful businessman doing business with call girls, John A is a middle-aged executive earning $25,000 a year. He is in the mass-communications media, works in midtown Manhattan, is happily married, but discovered eight years ago that he needed the additional companionship that call girls provide.

JOHN A: When I sit down for drinks with a girl, I don't have to do anything but talk about me. The real me. Who I am, how I feel. There's no talk about the mortgage or the problems with the kids. I see a certain girl once a week.

AUTHORS: Here in New York?

A: Yes. I go to her apartment.

AUTHORS: How much do you pay her?

A: I usually give her fifty dollars, but I sometimes take her a gift. Nothing extravagant.

AUTHORS: Do you feel guilty, in effect, cheating on your wife?

A: My wife is well taken care of. I love her, perhaps more than when we married.

AUTHORS: Are you bored with your sexual life at home?

A: There is a certain routine about it.

AUTHORS: And with your call girl?

A: There always seems to be something new and exciting.

AUTHORS: Things you might not care to do with your wife?

A: I guess you could say that.

AUTHORS: Have you been seeing this same girl all these eight years?

A: No. There have been several over the years. One introduces me to another. The girl I see now I've known for about a year.

AUTHORS: Many men at the point where they feel bored at home find another woman and have an affair rather than deal with a call girl. Why didn't you?

A: Too risky, I suppose. I live in a small suburban town. Word would get out, I'm sure. I don't want a deep emotional involvement with another woman.

AUTHORS: So it's purely for sex that you deal with call girls?

A: Yes, but it goes beyond that. You get to know each other, and you become friends of a kind.

John B:

A young executive on his way up in the brokerage business, John B has only recently been dealing with call girls. Because he has a special preference sexually, he finds that a call-girl relationship is the only way at the moment to fulfill that need.

JOHN B: I dig watching. So, I usually pay for two girls at once. They perform together for a while, and then I take part. Threesies, as they say.

AUTHORS: How often do you do this?

B: Not as much as I'd like. It gets a little expensive, and I don't make that much.

AUTHORS: How much do you pay?

B: About a hundred dollars for both girls. Fifty each.

AUTHORS: Did you ever ask yourself why you like to watch a lesbian relationship?

B: What I'm watching is two women. I think the female body is beautiful. I like to watch women.

AUTHORS: What do you do with both girls when you get into the act?

B: The usual things. Oral sex with them and they on me. Then I usually settle with one and lay her. The other girl just sort of helps out. Petting and stroking and kissing. That sort of thing.

AUTHORS: Did you ever consider asking your wife to take part in a threesome? Group sex?

B: I have been thinking about that lately. I guess I'm too shy.

John C:

Like the harried husbands of the TV situation comedies, John C has a basically unhappy home life because he feels trapped by a demanding wife and a large family. A self-made man in the clothing retailing business, John C feels that he is largely unappreciated at home while beset by sometimes overwhelming problems. His wife of 30 years has no interest in sex.

C: She's a good woman and has been a wonderful wife. She's a fine mother to our kids. But she has her house and kids and TV to keep her busy.

AUTHORS: You've been dealing with call girls for fifteen years?

C: It started as a sometime thing. I found these young girls were interested in me and in seeing that I had a good time. I see a girl at least once a week now. I think it makes me a better man at home. I'm not so grouchy all the time.

John D:

At 38, John D has been doing business on a regular basis with call girls for eight years. He has never been married and says he does not ever expect to be married because his health is such that he is extremely limited in how much social life he can undertake. A teacher specializing in handicapped children, he works from his home. When he

G: It varies. Usually I see a girl for a short period of time. I don't have that much time when I'm on these trips.

AUTHORS: How much do you pay?

G: As much as one hundred dollars. It comes out of my expense account.

AUTHORS: No one ever questioned you about it?

G: Who would question? Everyone does it. It's expected. The company knows that a certain amount of expense-account money goes to girls.

John H:

A highly successful business executive, John H heads a Midwestern corporation dealing in steel products. In addition to his $75,000 yearly salary he has stock options and expense accounts that raise his annual worth well over $100,000. He is almost the stereotype of the busy executive. He travels in a company jet, stays at the best hotels, and schedules call girls into his frequent junkets with the same efficiency that he schedules business meetings. He has an assistant who arranges for the girls.

AUTHORS: A person with that much knowledge could use it against you to get ahead in the business.

JOHN H: He is a very trustworthy man and knows that his future with our company is secure. He has excellent taste.

AUTHORS: Tell us about one of your arrangements.

H: In San Francisco, I always stay at the St. Francis. It's close to the business region of the city and is a fine hotel. My assistant books a room next to or near mine for himself. The young woman goes to that room rather than to mine.

AUTHORS: The company pays for all of this?

H: Oh, of course.

AUTHORS: Does the girl stay the night?

H: Rarely.

AUTHORS: What about other cities?

H: The arrangement is much the same.

AUTHORS: Does your assistant also have girls on the company tab?

H: I never thought about it. I assume so. He's entitled.

Most of the Johns interviewed for this book were interested in simple, straightforward intercourse with the call girls they hired. Those who expected more from the girl usually were willing to pay a premium price. Most of these men also indicated that they were interested in and expected to engage in oral sexual activity with the girls. The girls themselves state that oral sex is a standard fare between them and their clients. "The men like to do it to us," one reported, "and they all seem to like it when we use our mouths on them. I guess there are a lot of wives who just refuse to do it."

Another girl believes that the way she uses her mouth is vital to her success as a call girl. She says almost every John wants her to perform fellatio upon him. Some men want only that. "There are a thousand different ways of doing it orally," she concludes.

Many prostitutes feel that oral sex is preferable to regular intercourse. "It's faster and cleaner," one notes. Another girl said she could delight her clients by performing fellatio with warm water in her mouth. Another swears that she can assure herself of a repeat visit from the man by putting oil of wintergreen on her tongue before sucking him. "The men want to come back again and again. I never tell them what it was that made them feel so good."

When it comes to intercourse, it is important that the John feel he is satisfying the girl. "You have to be a real actress sometimes," says Platinum. "You've got to make the John feel as if he's really turning you on." She referred

approvingly to a scene in the film *Klute* in which Jane
Fonda plays a call girl. The scene shows her writhing in
obvious pleasure with a man only to glance at her wrist
watch momentarily before resuming her act.

All call girls who deal with men from the executive
suite feel that they have an obligation to make the client
as at ease and as comfortable as possible, helping him
when he's nervous or ill at ease, relaxing him, assuring
him that his every wish is her command. Platinum sums
it up: "You have to make this guy feel that he is the
greatest lover in the world and that he does to you what
no one else could ever do."

"A lot of times you start out pretending you mean it,"
says another girl, "and it winds up that you do. I know a
lot of Johns that I like a hell of a lot. They're nice men, and
I like being with them. Frankly, I wouldn't want to be in
any other business right now."

Most of the call girls interviewed related that their
Johns tend to be very shy or reticent at the first meeting.
"The girl very often has to take the initiative. She has to
get the man relaxed and to let him know that she's interested in what he's interested in," says one of the girls. "I
find a kiss is a good way to begin."

How the girl acts in the bedroom is important, they say.
Some prefer a slow and tantalizing approach, much like
stripteasing. Others are more direct, such as one girl who
always presents herself completely undressed to the man.
"It shakes a lot of them up. They expect to go through a
courtship or something, as if they were on a date. To come
into a room and find a gal lying there naked and ready and
waiting, well, it starts the action if nothing else."

When the girl gets paid is largely up to her. If she is
dealing directly with the man, she may want the cash
before. If she knows him or is sure of him, she may wait
until afterward.

Much is made of the role of the John in the illegality of

prostitution. There is a growing demand from Women's Liberation groups to prosecute the Johns as much as the women involved in the flesh trade. On this subject Judge Jack Rosenberg of the New York Criminal Court says, "The mere fact that Johns are willing victims (of an allegedly victimless crime) makes them nonetheless victims who are mulcted of their hard-earned money and exploited to their disadvantage by the people who live off them." The judge further believes that as a practical matter it would be difficult to prosecute Johns because the prostitutes involved do not come forward to testify. "The John is also the alleged victim, and most people would have sympathy for the John," the Judge concludes.

In a crackdown on a call-girl operation as a result of an investigation into police corruption in New York City, prosecutions of the Johns involved were generally dropped. One John arrested in a raid on the operation was an Ohio telephone executive accused of patronizing the house. All charges against the man were dismissed on the motion of the Manhattan district attorney. During the first five months of 1971, only 70 men were arraigned on charges of being Johns, while arraigned in the Manhattan criminal courts that same period were more than 3,000 women accused of prostitution. Most call girls believe that the John is not the one to be blamed (if anyone is to be blamed) for the hiring of prostitutes. Most say that they, the girls, are the ones breaking the law.

Today there is very little risk that a John will be arrested and even less chance that he will be prosecuted.

For the executive or otherwise successful or wealthy man there is always the possibility of blackmail. "It happens," a morals-squad detective reports. "I had one recently. There were no pictures or anything, but there was a long letter about where the girls lived and how much this guy paid. We have no way of knowing who may be paying a blackmailer, of course. It's best if the guy on the hook comes to us. Many are afraid to, of course."

The detective paused for a moment and toyed with some papers on his desk. Finally, he said, "I haven't been able to find any joy in what these people are involved in. To me there seems to be an awful lot of fear."

15

The Law

He tools around town in a customized T-bird that everyone recognizes as a "pimpmobile." He drives it because he likes flashy things and because it tells the world that this cat has made it, never mind that he made it in the flesh trade nor that what he is doing is illegal. Legalities are for the high-priced lawyers in his pay. Legalities are taken care of with payoffs—to cops and to judges. Money talks, and money is what this cat has. Never mind that he gets it from girls who work for him. The share of money he gets from the girls insures them against arrests and, failing that, from jail. It's the system. He didn't invent it. He just took advantage of it. As the ads say, "If you got it, flaunt it." The business is built on the payoff, and the pimp expects his share. The business thrives because it is illegal. That illegality is now under question, if not outright attack, due largely to the efforts of the Women's Liberation Movement.

"Prostitution is the symbol of the sexual exploitation of women," argues a Women's Liberation leader, "and if sexist exploitation of women is to cease in America, so must the system that makes criminals out of prostitutes who are, after all, the victims of a sexist society in the first place."

Author Kate Millet states that most of the "crap" that a prostitute has to take comes from the illegality of prostitution. "It seems to me that if we took it off the books we ought not institutionalize it. That acknowledges the right of the State to have a monopoly in the trade of persons which no State has the right to do," she states.

Another writer interested in the "decriminalization" of prostitution, Sanford H. Kadish, believes that the driving force behind prostitution laws is principally the conviction that prostitution is immoral. Writing in the *Annals of the American Academy of Political and Social Sciences*, Kadish says, "Although there are social harms beyond private immorality in commercialized sex—spread of venereal disease, exploitation of the young, and the affront of public solicitation, for example—the blunt use of the criminal prohibition has proven ineffective and costly. Prostitution has perdured in all civilizations; indeed, few institutions have proven as hardy. The inevitable conditions of social life unfailingly produce the supply to meet the ever-present demand. . . .

"To the extent that spread of venereal disease, corruption of the young, and public affront are the objects of prostitution controls, it would require little ingenuity to devise modes of social control short of the blanket criminalization of prostitution which would at the same time prove more effective and less costly for law enforcement. Apparently, the driving force behind prostitution laws is principally the conviction that prostitution is immoral. Only the judgement that the use of criminal law for verbal vindication of our morals is more important than its use to protect life and property can support the preservation of these laws as they are."

Nonetheless, prostitution is, at the moment, illegal, and

that is the basic fact of life for anyone who engages in it
—streetwalker, call girl, madam, secretary, corporate executive, or political leader. Because it is outside the law,
people who generally live within the law turn for help in
procuring the services of prostitutes to the procurer, the
pimp. There's always a middleman. They flourish in a
wide variety of species.

In the heady upper echelons of big business, the industrial pimp is likely to be known as a public-relations man.
He's the glad-hand Charley who gets tickets for the hottest show in town, the big fight, 50-yard-line seats for
pro-football playoffs, and the beauties for fun and games
in the executive suite. Call him what you will, or what *he*
will, he's a pimp. The name on the door and the Bigelow
on the floor are window dressing.

Also in the ranks of the business hierarchy are nonpaid
pimps, guys who have no title on their door but who
would like to. These are the office sharpies, like "Danny,"
mentioned earlier, who wheel and deal and come up with
cuties for those ranked above him on the corporate organizational charts. He does what he does in hopes of a promotion, a favor here and there, inclusion on the corporate
guest lists at parties, or just to be rubbing elbows with the
boss.

And then there are the guys who have a harem of girls
who work the streets and bars for them, the classic pimps
of the pool hall and sleazy hotel. These characters range
from two-bit bums supporting a drug habit to the decked-
out dude in the customized T-bird, the man at the top of
the heap, the cat who's got it made.

There can be a certain amount of upward mobility in
the life of the pimp, moving up from the streets to the ele-
gance of the man who handles high-priced girls for high-
paying customers. David Freeman, writing in *New York*
magazine, described one of the street pimps, a character named Lamont, who parlayed his girls and his busi-

or benefiting from it. These, however, were all mis-demeanor cases, relatively minor, with a maximum penalty of one year. More serious forms of pimping are classified as felonies, with sentences ranging from one to 17 years.

"These charges are lodged against pimps accused of controlling several prostitutes, promoting houses of prostitution or using under-age girls. But the most recent court figures show not a single felony conviction in 1967 or the first half of 1968.

"The police say that even if a prostitute testifies against a pimp, she still needs corroborating evidence, and this is difficult to obtain. Usually, arrests of pimps are made in connection with some act of violence.

"In adopting the 15-day law for prostitution, the Legislature also decided to decree punishment for the patron similar to that of the prostitute. The idea was that traffic might be curtailed because a man, especially if married, would think twice before patronizing a prostitute.

"Although policemen waiting outside hotels arrest alleged customers fairly regularly—112 in the first half of 1968—only one or two have been convicted. The usual defense is to admit nothing and to affirm that no prostitution was involved.

"Specialists such as Judge Basel disagree with those who would equate the prostitute and the customer, pointing out that the prostitute is in business—a hardened professional and often a recidivist.

"Although the police and lawyers agree that the largest number of girls now working the streets here are young —ranging from 17 to 23 years old—among those recently convicted here for prostitution were girls as young as 16 and a 71-year-old woman whose first brush with the law preceded Woodrow Wilson's election in 1912."

The 15-day law in New York State was roundly denounced by everyone, with the exception of the hookers and the pimps, and in April 1969, Governor Nelson A. Rockefeller announced that he had signed a bill changing the law to increase the maximum term for prostitution from 15 to 90 days, a law still considerably more lenient than the previous one that carried provisions for penalties up to one year in jail. The governor noted on signing the law that it represented "an interim attempt to deal with what appears to be a marked increase in the incidence of acts of prostitution in this State, particularly in the City of New York."

When the tougher law went into effect in September 1969, it made little noticeable dent in the traffic in New York City. The *Daily News* reported on October 6, 1969, that there was no effect on the prostitution population in the city. Pimps felt the pinch in their pockets, however, because judges set higher bails. By December 1969 the Public Morals Squad of the NYPD reported a decline in street activity by hookers. "A lot of girls are leaving town because they don't want to get ninety days or $500 fines," a Morals Squad cop stated. In February 1970 figures released by the police showed an increase in arrests again —7,877 female prostitutes in 1969—but by September 1970 the number of arrests was down by 18 percent.

Further pressure on the New York City authorities to curb prostitution occurred early in 1971 when the former West German defense minister, Franz Josef Straus, was mugged near the Plaza Hotel and an Italian industrialist was stabbed outside the Hilton Hotel—by prostitutes.

Yet despite the crackdown by the police, prostitution in midtown Manhattan remained a major problem—largely because of crimes associated with the activities of the girls. Then came what was for Manhattan pimps and their girls an infamous day. Hordes of hookers descended on a convention in a midtown hotel, besieging the conventioneers, plying their wares, and making general nuisances of themselves. But this was no ordinary convention. It was a meeting of the American Bar Association.

Next day as he strode into his courtroom in the Manhattan Criminal Court Building, Judge Morris L. Schwalb was incensed by what had happened at the Bar Association convention. Angrily claiming that "the midtown area is inundated with prostitution," Judge Schwalb ordered two women charged with prostitution held without bail. Two others were placed on extraordinarily high bail of $5,000 each. A court attendant cracked, "The pimps were fainting in the hallway."

Judge Schwalb found himself in the center of a storm. He was denounced by a group of 50 women for his decision to deny bail to the two women. One woman carried a placard outside his court stating: "Prostitution: Men's Crime Against Women."

It was a cry to be heard increasingly in the succeeding months. The thrust of the argument is that there *is* a victim in the crime of prostitution and that the victim is the prostitute. She is the victim, the argument goes, of a male, sexist society.

One of the organizers of a conference on prostitution held by various political and women's groups argued, "The prostitute is like the drug addict and is a victim. The pimp is a pusher and the solicitor is a pusher. They should be prosecuted and not the prostitute."

Prostitution, the women's activist groups state, is just one more example of the sexual suppression of women. It is the natural result of a society in which men have expected women to be subservient. It is the natural result of a society in which women are regarded as sex toys. Therefore, women who have become ensnared in this man-imposed system should not be regarded as criminals but as victims. Women who hold these views say that prostitution should be "decriminalized" rather than legalized. To legalize it, to institutionalize it, they say, would be simply to turn over to formal government functions the same depersonalization of womanhood that now exists.

Feminist Kate Millet believes that prostitutes already suffering as the victims of what is essentially a man's institution should not be expected to pay the price of the illegality of that institution, namely, "the harassment by the police, the shaking down by the judges, bribes from everybody—pimps, all the rest of it."

"If you are going to penalize anyone," suggests a New York feminist, "why penalize the woman? Penalize the pimp and customer. I would penalize only the third party —anyone making money off of this, off of two people having sexual congress."

All feminists agree that the idea that it's a "man's world" has fostered prostitution through the ages and does so today.

Leaders of the Women's Liberation Movement who advocate the "decriminalization" of prostitution argue that the armed forces foster prostitution by stationing American servicemen in areas where prostitution is either legal or accepted. At the conference on prostitution, Paula Conrad, a lawyer, stated, "We've taken a whole group of men and sent them to a culture alien to their own, and what we are teaching them is to use people as objects. We expose them to prostitution there. It's legalized. The Rest and Recreation areas are in Thailand, which has legal prostitution, or Japan, which had a thousand years of legal prostitution. We send them to Hong Kong. They come to Hawaii, which has massage parlors with the consent of the authorities. It's interesting that they don't like to go to Australia. It's different there. The freedom for licentiousness doesn't exist there. You can't divorce the problem of prostitution from the military."

The idea of "love 'em and leave 'em" and a "girl in

every port," say the Women's Liberationists, is fostered by the military with the effect that GIs returning home are corrupted by the idea that women are sex objects.

That there are prostitutes available to GIs stationed overseas is nothing new, nor is the phenomenon peculiar to Americans. There have always been camp followers, and there are today. A young marine writing to the authors from Okinawa described the locale around Camp Butler and the nearest big city, Koza, as "full of bars, steam baths, and whorehouses."

Claiming that the military is aware of the financial aspects of prostitution near U.S. bases, Paula Conrad reported, "I spoke to someone in the Defense Department who explained to me that the official policy was to place off-limits any house of prostitution. However, they felt they couldn't do this in Germany or other places because they would violate the sovereignty of that nation. But what they didn't mention was that every time the fellows in Boston or in California want to get a good contract they take out the generals and the civilian employees of the various government-procurement offices and provide them with call girls. While they are willing to lock up their own men, and they do, officers are very rarely treated that way. In Vietnam they had two sets of brothels. One for officers and one for enlisted men."

While large institutions bear some of the brunt of the blame by the feminists for the institution of prostitution, it is the pimp who reaps a harvest of scorn from the women. He is a man who either sells girls to others for a share of the money or who lives off a girl who does her own soliciting. "I hate pimps," says Platinum. "I can't stand pimps. I heard so much about these guys when I was first starting on my own, so I said to myself that if this is the 'in' thing, let me try it. I went from one who was kind —he never touched me, never laid a glove on me. He was so slick. He wants to get an apartment. He wants to get my clothes together. He wants to get his clothes together. He wants to be top man in his profession. He's nothing. He's an absolute nothing. Every night I would come in and give him a hundred or a hundred and fifty dollars, and next morning he was broke. It dawned on me that he had to be either using it for—I didn't know what—or blowing it some place. I found he would take the money I gave him and go to a dope house and put it all in snow or cocaine."

Prostitution researcher Dr. Harold Greenwald writes, "A common myth is that the pimp is selected by the call girl because of his superior sexual prowess. The myth is based on the old belief that prostitutes in general are over-sexed and that when they find a man who can fill their sexual needs, as their clients cannot, they are willing to shower on him all the money they earn in gratitude for his great sexual potency. There seems to be very little basis in fact for this myth. While it is true that call girls frequently found themselves able to have more satisfactory or, at least, less unsatisfactory physical relationships with pimps than with clients, few of them spoke of their pimps as being great lovers."

The relationship seems to be an emotional one. The girl needs the pimp, if for nothing else, to keep her from being lonely. That, say the feminists, is the grossest kind of male exploitation and why the pimp is the criminal, not the girl.

In answer to that premise, sociologist Charles Winick of the City College of the City University of New York, author of *The Lively Commerce, Prostitution in the United States*, says even if pimps were to be prosecuted it would be a nearly impossible task because the girls would be reluctant to testify against them.

"If we could get prostitutes to testify against pimps and other exploiters in the courts, that would be very good. Then we could address ourselves to implementing the laws against abuses such as blackmail, forced labor, and the like rather than regulating the mere sale of sex.

"But in fact because of the emotional ties which prostitutes have with pimps and similar persons, it is almost impossible to get a prostitute to testify against a pimp even after he has rejected her, beat her up, thrown her out, taken all her money and will not even talk to her.

"So, in principle, we should have laws regulating the exploitation of these women, but we know that such laws would not be enforceable because it is important to the woman to be beaten, assaulted, have her money taken away, be supplied with heroin, and so forth. These are part of her complicated emotional relationship with her pimp.

"So if we eliminated the laws against prostitution and encouraged police to implement the laws against exploitation, nothing would happen."

Professor Winick suggests that the remedy for prostitution is neither legal nor psychological but social in nature. He suggests that we should recognize that prostitutes, like drug addicts, are a large group of people who are in great difficulty and are unable to adapt in a conventional way. He says what is needed is a program of resocialization to give these women a feeling of confidence in themselves in group living. The prostitute, he says, should be taught to get along with other people and to move into a more acceptable way of life in society without being stigmatized or without requiring her to be further degraded by becoming an informer. He laments the fact that no community in the United States has such a program.

Whether the way we deal with prostitution will be through legalization, decriminalization, resocialization, or some other means remains to be seen. The only thing clear in the current debate over prostitution in our society is that something is going to be done eventually but that a good deal of debating and discussing will occur first.

The solution at the moment seems beyond everyone's vision.

Even Reverend Billy Graham when visiting in disguise —and strictly as an observer—a red-light district in Amsterdam, the Netherlands, had to struggle with the question of what to do about the "oldest profession." "I was inclined to stand in the middle of the street and shout, 'People, there is salvation for you! God loves you!,' " he recalled. "I didn't do it. After all, it wasn't a suitable occasion."

blue paper and was prepared to deposit the ad in the corner trash basket. Instead, he read the ad twice.

STUDIO 34

The Miracle on 34th Street

My name is Lisa, and I am just one of five young, attractive girls who will give you a very relaxing and unforgettable massage in our studio, so if you are in New York just for a short stay, or you live in New York, become a regular.

Stan pushed the ad into his coat pocket and continued on to his office, his mind turning over the idea of spending his lunch hour at the massage studio. For Stan and thousands of others in New York and other major cities the massage parlor offering relaxing "massage" by pretty young girls is the newest wrinkle in the mushrooming business of sex and sexual excitement for profit in the United States.

Massage parlors are old hat in other parts of the world. They abound in the Far East. They first put in an appearance in the United States in California and quickly became a thriving business. The first parlors opened in New York in 1967. They have since become going concerns in other areas and are even cropping up in smaller cities and larger towns from coast to coast.

The ads offer the relaxation of massage, but between the lines in the advertisements is the expectation that there will be more than the usual back rub with oil or talcum. The allure is sex, and often that is precisely what the customer gets—if he pays a little extra.

Leaving his office a little after noon, Stan Hunter headed along Thirty-fourth Street in search of the massage studio named in the advertisement. With a little hesitation, he pushed open the door and walked in. . . .

Reporter Donald Singleton in the *New York Daily News* wrote: "The places are called massage studios, but what goes on in them is often against the law, even though the technicalities prevent police from making arrests. A decade ago, the sudden proliferation of massage studios here might have touched off a wave of public outrage. Now only a few voices are raised against them, and rather calmly." In New York in 1971 only eight arrests were made for prostitution in the massage parlors in the city, while in that same period, according to police, about 40 of the studios opened for business. The businesses flourished because of a change in the laws and regulations that revoked the requirement of licenses to operate such establishments.

"Many of the parlors opened in midtown areas near the large office buildings and made open appeals to prospective clients to spend a relaxing lunch hour under the rubbing, probing, kneading hands of attractive women. Thousands of young businessmen accepted the invitations. The parlors varied in appearance and style, ranging from shoestring operations in storefronts to sumptuous establishments complete with saunas and the most modern equipment. Always, the lure—held out indirectly—was that sex was the commodity for sale."

Stan Hunter is now a devoted customer of massage salons, spending at least one lunch hour a week in one of the establishments in midtown Manhattan. He has tried several of them and among these found a few that satisfied him. But they went out of business, as the massage parlors frequently do. He now visits one that shows some signs of permanence. It is modern and comfortable. The walls of the reception room are hung with official-looking documents and diplomalike certificates. The floor is carpeted.

The man at the desk—the manager—is young, hip-looking but neat and well-mannered. He knows Stan now and trusts him. At first the manager and the girls were suspicious, expecting that the lean young man might be a police officer. His first experience involved a massage—nothing more. The shapely young woman who gave it to him seemed to know what she was doing. Stan felt quite relaxed. The first time he made no overtures about receiving something extra. On his second visit, as he lay on his back on the massage table, his penis erect, he muttered a few words about how great it would be if he "could get a hand job." The masseuse smiled and lowered her eyelids demurely. "That is against the rules," she whispered in a husky voice. "Who's gonna know?" Stan said with a little laugh. He waited. Nothing happened. "Not even for a little extra tip?" he asked. The young woman shrugged. "Well," she said, smiling, "I guess it would be all right." With that, Stan closed his eyes and let the young woman lead him to a spectacular climax. On his next visit, Stan was less shy. "That was great the last time," he said to the young woman, "but do you know what I'd really like? Some head." For a ten-dollar tip, Stan went back to his office totally relaxed. On his lunch hour he had spent $27. The visit to the parlor cost him $17. The extra attention by his masseuse, another $10. "Hell, I'd spend nearly that much on drinks and lunch, anyway," he cracks, "and probably put on a few ounces. This way, I get some pleasure, feel genuinely relaxed, and watch my weight."

Of the money Stan pays for his weekly visit to the massage parlor, the young masseuse gets to keep the $10 with no kickback to the management. She gets a share of the $17 fee collected by the establishment.

A massage parlor visited by the authors exhibited the following price chart:

Massage $15
Body-painting $17
Photography $13 (for half hour)

A young woman working undercover for the authors visited this establishment to be interviewed for a job as a masseuse. Located on the second floor of a run-down building in midtown Manhattan, the massage parlor was a small establishment—a large reception room–office, three cubicles to the rear of the location, and a sauna. "To me it looked like a five-dollar whorehouse," the undercover girl reported. "The place really doesn't impress you."

Equally unimpressive was the "sleazy character" who interviewed her. "He was very shaky, very unsure of himself. He asked if I ever worked in a massage parlor before. I told him I hadn't. Then he proceeded to ask us what days we'd be free to work. He told us what we were expected to do—hand massage and heterosexual activity. I asked if photography was allowed. He said it was but no hard-core stuff, no penetration of any kind. He assumed that we would have no objections to that. It was clear that it was expected of us. Of the fifteen dollars, I would get four dollars plus whatever tips I got."

The interviewer stated that a girl could make $200 to $300 a week. "I doubt that," commented the undercover girl. "You would have to knock down twenty to thirty guys a day. That's a lot of people to massage at thirty-five minutes per session."

In virtually all of these establishments it is the customer who must raise the subject of sexual activity. If the girl were to do it, she would be liable to a charge of solicitation for prostitution. Arrests, however, are rare. In August 1971, New York police did make arrests at two massage locations when a policewoman posing as a prostitute applied for a job at one of the establishments and was hired allegedly with the expectation that she was to engage in prostitution. A member of the New York Police Department Morals Squad discussed the massage-parlor business with the authors:

SERGEANT: I can tell you specifically about an arrest I made that resulted in two convictions, the manager for promoting prostitution and the girl for prostitution. I went in the first time on a Monday, and the manager took me aside and searched me. He said he had to be sure I wasn't a cop or a psycho. Then the girl came in and gave me a massage. She wouldn't do anything else because she said she couldn't be sure I wasn't a cop. The second time I went back I went through the same routine. The third time, she knew me. I also took along my hack license (I drive a cab part-time). I saw the big sign on the wall that said tipping was allowed. I told her I was prepared to give her a tip. I asked her what did she do and how much. As I recall she wanted thirty dollars for a fellatio. I placed her under arrest then and there. She cried for forty-five minutes. She was really a pitiful thing. Lots of bad things had happened to her. Among all the other things, she was brought to a massage studio on the West Side, and the manager or the owner of that studio took her into the back room and fornicated with her, had pictures taken of the act while making love. After that he tried to talk her into working there. He had one of the girls take her into a room while she had a customer there and teach this young kid how to fellate.
AUTHORS: What kind of girls do you find in these places?
SERGEANT: Most of them are hard. Hookers. But there was one place on the East Side where the girls were absolutely beautiful. All European girls, just delightful. They were professional masseuses, and we were told that they would not do anything but give massages. It's too bad because my partner and I had just gotten some back pay

and we had lots of bread on us. Those girls were so great I think we would have had a ball. And no arrests.

When arrests are made, the customers are generally not taken in. Charges are filed against the operators of the establishments and the employees, but the chances of arrest remain small and the noontime customer can feel certain that he will not be caught in a headline-making scandal.

When arrests are made, they splash into the headlines. Recently, a massage establishment called Executive Relaxation set up shop in Hicksville, Long Island. With considerable fanfare, the establishment advertised a series of "sneak previews" of the handsomely appointed facilities on the third floor of a building in the New York City suburb. Guests entered a lounge whose floor and walls were carpeted in pink. From the lounge customers were escorted to a bar for free drinks and hors d'oeuvres. A fee of $25 was required as an "entrance fee." Once paid, customers were invited to choose their girls and to follow them to six private massage rooms where the gals helped the men to luxurious baths in sunken Grecian tubs. The girls wore leotards and pantyhose. The leotards were discarded as they stepped into showers to help the men rinse after their baths. At this point, according to Nassau County District Attorney William Cahn, the girls negotiated "extracurricular" activities.

Cahn learned of the operation by sending undercover agents to the sneak previews. Cahn then waited for the grand opening of the massage parlor. When the doors opened officially, Cahn's men went back to the establishment and raided it. A newspaper reported that "six sheepish 'executives' were allowed to put on their clothes and depart." Cahn's detectives arrested two men, allegedly the managers of Executive Relaxation, and six girls. The two men were charged with promoting prostitution.

The girls were charged with loitering or prostitution.

Some of the better-organized operations feel it is in their interest to offer their services away from their studios and parlors. Girls go out to private homes and hotels carrying their massage equipment in make-up cases or overnight bags and perform their services wherever their appointments are. There is a great deal of risk of arrest in these situations. A New York City detective described one such situation:

DETECTIVE: We obtained a leaflet advertising residential massage featuring Swedish or Danish, French, or Japanese massage. It gave a phone number. I called, and it was answered by a male. He filled me in on the facts. It would have to be in Manhattan in my own apartment or hotel. I told him I'd just arrived from out of town and hadn't checked into a hotel yet but I had reservations. He told me to call him when I was checked in. I made an arrangement with a hotel to lend me a room. I called the massage service and told the guy where I was staying. He then called me back to verify it. I made arrangements to have a girl come to my room at one in the afternoon. I waited. I took off my shirt and shoes and had the TV on to make it look legitimate. At one o'clock a girl came, a very young girl, attractive, blonde. She lit a cigarette and made small talk for a while until she was convinced I was on the up-and-up. She called the guy back and said I looked okay. She wanted her money first. I asked her about the three types of massage. The prices were thirty-five, forty, and fifty dollars. I said I'd go for the fifty-dollar massage, but I asked her to explain to me what the three types were. She said the Danish is done by hand. I asked if they weren't all done by hand. She said they weren't. She said the French is done a different way. French is fellatio, she explained to me. Japanese is combination fellatio and lay. I asked her if that's what I'd paid for. She said it was unless

I wanted something else. I said, "No, that's all right, but before we go any further, I'm a police officer and you are under arrest."

In this, her first arrest, the young woman pleaded guilty in night court and was fined $50. She told the arresting officer she was 21 years old. He surmised she was younger. At the time of her arrest she had in her possession no equipment, massagers, or oils that would at least give her the appearance of being a legitimate masseuse.

DETECTIVE: We busted her the next night. My partner was set up in a hotel and this girl came—with a massage kit. She laughed and told him how she had been arrested the night before. My partner went along with her, laughing and joking, and then he says, "You won't believe this, but—" This time she pleaded guilty again and was fined seventy-five dollars.

On the basis of these two arrests and the telephone conversation with the man running this traveling massage business, the detectives obtained search warrants, visited the apartment where the man conducted his business, arrested him, and charged him with promoting prostitution.

When making arrests of girls in these circumstances, members of the New York City Police Department are not permitted to disrobe below the waist. The girls who work the massage businesses know these regulations and do not—unless they are very foolhardy—engage in any prostitution with a man who is not fully unclothed. "A cop can't bust you if he's naked," a massage girl jokes.

Another member of the morals squad relates a case history of a young woman arrested for prostitution under the guise of massage:

DETECTIVE: This girl told me she had been a model and had been solicited by the wife of the guy she was working for. This guy had an operation using three girls. This girl, another one, and his wife. She had been doing it for three months, and it was her first arrest. A lot of the massage girls when they're busted are busted for the first time. Street girls tend to have records.

There are many dodges used by the operators of the massage establishments to avoid being liable for prosecution under the laws against promoting prostitution. The objective is to make the girls as legally responsible as possible. The young woman who acted as an undercover operative for the authors in this and other aspects of the "sex-in-the-executive-suite syndrome" was interviewed by a massage and artist studio as "an independent contractor." In effect, the girl was contracting for space in the establishment rather than being an employee. She was required to sign a statement to that effect. Excerpts of the form are reproduced below:

XXXXXX Massage Studio

Dated_____

I, _____, residing at _____ hereby apply for work-space rental, services and facilities offered to free-lance models by the above STUDIO, under the following conditions:

  1. I hereby warrant that I am an independent contractor working my own business as a free-lance model, and it is specifically understood and agreed that I am not employed by the above studio in any manner, directly or indirectly. . . .

2. I hereby further agree to save harmless the above STUDIO, its officers and employees, for any photograph, sketch, movies, printed matter, or advertising copy, etc., etc., whether released or unreleased, made by any artist or photographer while using my services at the above premises. . . .

RULES AND REGULATIONS:

A. I will at all times pose in an artful and decent manner and will never pose for any lewd, lascivious, or indecent photograph, movie, sketch, drawing, or painting.
B. I will never permit any photographer or artist to touch my person, nor will I touch myself in any manner degrading to the art of modeling while on the premises of the above studio. . . .

Besides the massage parlors operating from a fixed location, there are many individuals who set themselves up in business and who give these "complete body massages" and offer "total relaxation" in their apartments or through "residential service." These are free-lancers, almost none of whom have had any training whatsoever in massage. Their commodity is sex and little else. One of these is a young Canadian named Tony. He operates a service in association with his girl friend Therese. He services hetero- and homosexual clients, has a compact work kit including various kinds of massagers, and charges upwards of $35 a visit. He has a handful of men whom he visits at their offices. These are all successful businessmen with a homosexual preference. Tony was once a male prostitute but has gone into the massage business rather than working the streets. He and Therese occasionally work together.

In large cities a great deal of homosexual prostitution poses under the banner of the massage business. These massage services are nothing more than call-boy operations designed for the executive or prominent man who must guard against public disclosure of his sexual preference. Advertisements appearing in underground newspapers offering "rubdowns for men" are usually covers for homosexual prostitution services that operate along the same lines as call-girl services with comparable price lists. There are established massage parlors that also cater to the male with a desire for a "complete body massage" by a young and attractive boy.

A writer in *Screw* claimed that half of the more than 40 massage establishments operating in Manhattan were serving gay clientele exclusively.

This same writer gave some advice to the bone-weary male looking for the complete relaxation of the massage parlor. "Hotels should be avoided, as well as large operations which offer such unrelated options as swimming pools, karate lessons, squash courts, Mah-Jong tournaments, whatever."

That the all-over, complete body massage is a rapidly growing part of the executive's routine was evident recently in London. All over the city, stickers pasted on billboards and inside telephone booths announced, "Sonya gives full body massage." A telephone number was listed. For days the phone rang with customers interested in what Sonya had to offer. The phones belonged to Intourist, the travel agency of the Soviet Union. The Committee of Fighters for Soviet Jewry, an underground group, took the credit by calling British newspapers to announce that it was the Sonya in the ads.

17

Marty's
Escort Service

> We already know you are an Angel, but here's a chance to be a devil, too!
>
> You are cordially invited to attend a backers' party previewing what we are sure will be next season's biggest hit on Broadway.
>
> Come hear the music and all about the show.
>
> We guarantee you, this will be the most unusual backers' party you've ever attended!

The invitations, which went to wealthy persons who had previously invested money in theatrical enterprises, listed an address and an apartment for the party that was being held by two young men who had just written a musical comedy that they wished to produce.

Their plan was to treat their potential backers to an orgy.

To arrange the details the two innovative showmen hired Marty's Escort Service to provide everything they would need for a successful party. "We provided the music, of course, from the score of our show," one of the bright young men said with a smile as he explained the details of this unusual entertainment for the invited "angels." The apartment for the orgy was provided by Marty. He also supplied girls and arranged the catering of food and drink. Because some wealthy women were to be invited, Marty also arranged for a handful of young men to provide whatever special services the moneyed ladies might require. As the guests entered the apartment, they were met by an appropriate date—girls for the men, boys for the women, and, in one case, a boy for a man. These charming young escorts wore bikini bathing suits as they greeted the guests who were promptly invited to put their coats and all their clothing aside. Nude, fed, and wined, the guests listened to the score of the show. It was a fine property, they agreed. They applauded warmly, and as the hosts passed out blank checks and pens, the "angels" pledged their money. With business out of the way and plenty of money raised, the hosts and guests settled into an evening of uninhibited sex.

The show was a hit for two seasons and launched the young showmen onto a career that is so successful that they no longer need the gimmick of an orgy to raise backing for their ventures.

Of all his undertakings, Marty most often tells this story of the orgy that paved the way for a Broadway hit, but he has files filled with other tales of how he helped arrange an evening of enjoyment through his escort service. "My girls are high-class," he boasts. He exhibits a photograph of one of his most successful employees, a young woman named Gloria.

Through sunglasses, Gloria Martin, a beautiful young woman of 23, half-awake, half-asleep, looked down on a swimming pool in a city park far below her terrace. She watched some boys splashing noisily, and she longed for a swim. Her wrist watch told her she would have to hurry or be late for her date. Sighing for the pleasures lost to adults, she adjusted the glasses on her straight nose, pushed herself up from her chaise lounge, and went into her apartment to dress for the date. She slipped out of her summery dress and stood naked before her mirror, striking a pose she saw in fashion magazines. Her body was much fuller than those of the gaunt girls in the magazines, and as she touched her large breasts, lifting them in her cupped hands, although they needed no lift, she felt a surge of satisfaction with her figure. Half an hour later, showered, lightly made up, and wearing a cool but chic dress with a single strand of pearls, she rode to the lobby in a cool elevator, strode breezily through the lobby with a nod to the handsome doorman, and stepped into a waiting limousine. The young driver gave her a wink. "Always on time, Gloria," he smiled.

"Where are we going?" she asked brightly.

"Casey's. Your date is waiting there now. I just dropped him off."

Occupying a corner of First Avenue in the Sixties, Casey's was a saloon. An authentic landmark of New York, it was unlikely that Casey's would receive a plaque from the landmark-preservation association, yet it had stood on this corner for years and seen a good deal of New York's history. Once only a neighborhood bar, it had been bought by a pair of enterprising young men who transformed it into one of the earliest establishments of that phenomenon of New York in the sixties, the singles' bar. It was one of the world-famous spas where single women could be met by attractive young men. Entering Casey's,

Gloria was not available for one of those often interesting pickups. Instead, she searched the early-summer evening crowd for an older man described by the young driver of her limousine as medium in height, a shade on the heavy side, thinning on the top, and wearing a blue-striped summer-weight suit. Gloria spotted him immediately. She recognized him from a date the previous summer. She recalled that he was a businessman from Pennsylvania and a gentleman. He was one of Marty's best customers. She greeted him with a lighthearted "Hi." Typically, he rose to greet her. His name was Albert.

Gloria and Albert had two drinks at Casey's, crossed town in the limousine to the theater district, watched the city's hottest musical, dined after the show, then rode in the limousine to an apartment off Sutton Place.

"Marty hasn't changed this place very much," Albert observed as they entered the luxurious apartment. "You haven't changed much, either, Gloria," he added with a chuckle.

"Not at all," said Gloria, stepping into Albert's arms to kiss him on the mouth.

"Want another drink, or shall we . . . ?"

"I vote for 'shall we,' " she smiled, stroking her long fingers down Albert's chest. Turning and taking his hand, she led him to the bedroom. An air conditioner whirred softly in the dimly lighted room. The soft yellow light painted shadows upon the hills and valleys of Gloria's body as she slipped out of her dress and into bed. Albert nervously undressed and sat beside her.

"You are looking especially delicious tonight," Albert said hoarsely.

"Ooo, that sounds suggestive," Gloria sighed. She put a hand on Albert's feverish forehead. "You remembered what I like."

"How could I forget?" he laughed.

He said nothing more for a long time.

In the morning he telephoned Marty. "It was perfect as usual. Gloria is a lovely girl."

"Yes, she is," said Marty through the telephone. "Shall I make a reservation for you for your next visit?"

Albert's laugh boomed down the line. "Of course. Of course."

Gratified that his customer was pleased, Marty put down the phone only to answer its ring again a moment later with a cheery, "Marty's Escort Service, may we help you to an exciting date?"

The paid escort is nothing new, but its use has become more widespread in the years since World War II. Many of the escort or dating services are fronts for executive prostitution. Marty, a veteran of the Korean War, made a thorough study of escort services before going into the business himself. Observing the legitimate dating and escort services that were available in major American cities as well as those that were merely façades for call-girl services, Marty decided his service would not draw the line at providing sexual entertainment. "A guy goes on a date with a chick and expects to get something more out of it than a handshake when the date is over," he insists. And he is right. Implicit in virtually every call to Marty's service by prospective clients was the additional service his girls would be expected to provide. A typical client operates a public-relations service in New Jersey. The client telephoned Marty "out of the blue." Smiling, Marty explained, "We have an ad in the Yellow Pages. This PR guy got us from there. He let his fingers do the walking." Marty burst into laughter. "The guy didn't come right out and say he wanted to get his clients laid. He hinted at it. I told him to write me a letter on his stationery. He did. Then he followed up with a call."

The telephone call was recorded by the authors:
CLIENT: What's the situation?

MARTY: Your letter says you are interested in dates for two clients of yours, is that right?

CLIENT: Yes.

MARTY: Where will they be staying?

CLIENT: The Americana.

MARTY: Do you have their names?

CLIENT: I don't have their names yet. They're from out of town and are customers of a client of mine. I will have the names in a few days.

MARTY: Oh, all right. So, they'll be in here this coming Wednesday.

CLIENT: I'll have the names Wednesday. They'll be in the following week, the eleventh, twelfth, thirteenth, and possibly the fourteenth.

MARTY: Okay, so what you do is give me a call on the eleventh.

CLIENT: I want to find out what this is going to cost.

MARTY: How many are there?

CLIENT: It will be two, probably on the twelfth, a Saturday.

MARTY: You figure two clients?

CLIENT: Yes. They'll be in separate rooms, of course.

MARTY: That will be ninety dollars for two of 'em.

CLIENT: Now, everything will be taken care of?

MARTY: Right.

CLIENT: Okay, so I'll contact you.

MARTY: When they come in to the Americana. Who's paying for this?

CLIENT: I'll pay for it, and I'll be reimbursed by the company.

MARTY: All right. You'll have to mail it in to me before the date. You mail it in and I'll set it up for that Saturday.

CLIENT: For how long is this?

MARTY: There wouldn't be any time limit.

CLIENT: This is for the whole night?

MARTY: There wouldn't be any time limit.

CLIENT: You know what we're talking about? I'd really like to get down to business.

MARTY: I'll take care of it. I'll make the arrangements.

CLIENT: You'll make the arrangements, and the ninety dollars is for the two gentlemen.

MARTY: Right.

CLIENT: Okay. I'll call you and let you know their rooms at the Americana.

Through the veiled references both Marty and the client knew that they were discussing the obtaining of prostitutes for the men who were coming to the city. The price quoted was that for the sexual services of the women whom Marty would provide, but the price quoted was for the girls only. Marty's service would also include a charge for his arranging the deal and limousine service if desired. The cost of these dates would also involve dinner, drinks, tips, and the cost of theater tickets, if that was what the visiting gentlemen wished. "The ninety dollars is for the lay," Marty explains with a wink. "There are a few extras, the window dressing, the appearance of legitimacy, so to speak."

The girls themselves can add to the cost of their services. They call it "tipping," but it amounts to an extra charge for anything special a client may wish. Mary, a statuesque and buxom redhead, explains, "The fee that Marty quotes to a client is for a lay only. If the client wants a little more, the little extras that we can provide—fellatio, a party of two or three girls, a show of some kind—all that is extra. Tips."

Like the "extras" in massage establishments, the "extras" offered by the escort girls can amount to considerably more money than the fee originally quoted.

The advertising literature of the escort services is as subtle as possible while still getting across its message. "Any service you could possibly require," states one brochure. Others advertise special arrangements for apartments rather than hotel rooms. Parties can be peopled with "beautiful girls who know how to please." The brochures offer close-up photos of the girls but also display pictures of them in skimpy bathing suits.

The arrangements made by Marty on the telephone with the above client were finalized. A check arrived well in advance of the appointed date. The client called again with the names and room numbers of the men he wanted entertained. They were middle-aged men from a steel company in the Midwest. The evening included drinks at their hotel with the girls, Marty's limousine service to a showing of *Oh! Calcutta!,* a late supper at an uptown restaurant, drinks in the cocktail lounge of their hotel, and the rest of the night in bed with the girls.

Mary, laughing and tossing back her red hair, said of the date, "These men were horny, of course, but they really didn't have all that much staying power. It was a fast lay for each of them, and then they were sleeping away like babies. Many of these men talk a lot about how they're going to lay us all night long, but nine times out of ten it's over fast and they're sound asleep."

Asked about what seemed to us to be a rather low price for the services of the girls, Marty shrugged and said he did a large volume of business. "It's like any other business. You do a big turnover at a lower price and you rake in the dough."

Many escort services charge considerably more than Marty and deal with an affluent selected clientele who can afford the $100 to $500 a night demanded.

Another aspect of the escort or dating-service business is the arranging of parties at which numerous men are to be serviced. Stag parties, office smokers, and "orgies" are arranged by large firms seeking to entertain entire staffs of salesmen, buyers, or other important clients. These affairs require topless waitresses, dancers, hostesses, and companions for the men attending. When Marty is called on to arrange one of these large entertainments, he often engages the help of one of the city's madams. The party itself is usually held at the madam's apartment. "These are the affairs where late at night the lights go down low, the music is soft, and the guys end up fucking the chicks on the floor, standing up, in armchairs, on the couches, and even on the kitchen table. They're drunken orgies, is what they are."

A wealthy Manhattan financier with a summer house on Fire Island throws one of these parties every season. Using Marty's service to engage girls, he spends thousands of dollars for one evening. His clients, friends, and neighbors look forward to the party every year. "It usually comes near the end of the season just before the guy closes up his house for the winter," Marty reports.

While these special affairs are exciting and interesting as well as challenging, Marty and his competitors in the escort-service business obtain most of their income from the solitary gentleman or small groups of men visiting the big city and desiring the company of beautiful women as they do the town.

"For the guy who doesn't know who the madams are, won't risk picking up girls off the street, and doesn't have time to waste picking up chicks, the escort service is the answer," says Marty. "It's an easy and safe way to have a good time on a date and a good lay afterwards."

18

Group Sex and the
Executive Suite

"Group sex is primarily an experience to bring adventure, to satisfy curiosity and to perk up the increasingly routine sexual relationships that are so common to many of today's marriages," says Bud Corwin, a "swinger." With a smile and a wink, he adds, "There's also profit in it."

Bud Corwin is a 38-year-old businessman in Massachusetts. He operates a specialized secretarial service for prominent doctors and attorneys in Boston. While Bud's motives for becoming a "swinger" were strictly for personal adventure, he found that during his first year as a swinger his business prospered, growing more than 25 percent.

When Bud and his wife Sally formed their own swingers' club, Bud took charge of handling the membership rolls. He assured all newcomers that he would be very discreet, never giving out phone numbers directly, but acting as a contact himself between interested couples. Bud gave those same assurances to a man who called one day wanting information about the group, which he had heard about from one of the members. He was anxious that his participation be strictly confidential. "In my business, I have to be careful about this kind of thing," he said nervously. Bud assured the caller that all the members had similar feelings and that the man could be assured of utter discretion. When the man learned that Bud had a secretarial service in Boston, he laughed. It so happened that this man, a doctor, had just finished a paper that he was to present at a medical seminar and he was trying to find an efficient secretarial service to work on the paper for him. Bud had his first client via his swinging group. Bud's business income increased 25 percent (see chart) in the first year that he and Sally were social and sexual swingers.

Janette Benton is a 36-year-old college-educated piano teacher from a Chicago suburb. Janette and her husband Ron entered into the new swinging life with zest. Janette placed a classified advertisement in her local newspaper soliciting "modern couples" to join them in seeking friendship. She listed her home telephone number. Soon the entire neighborhood, including the parents of most of her young piano students, knew of Jan and Ron's sexual life.

At first Jan feared that she would lose her business, but of the 32 students, only two mothers questioned Jan about her morality. The buxom blonde piano teacher related the conversation:

STUDENT'S MOTHER: Jan [in shocked tone], how could you do such a thing? It's animalistic!
JAN: Ron and I were looking for compatibility and an intimate relationship with people that would be intellectually equal. We sought people that we would like being with and also have very good sex with. We don't have wall-to-wall mattresses. Nothing ever happens in our

home when I am giving piano lessons. This is our private life.
STUDENT'S MOTHER: I can understand if you fall in love with somebody and you really desire a man and you go to bed with him but this swinging is wrong.

Jan continued the discussion for nearly an hour with the questioning mother finally saying, "I guess it might be good for you if that's your thing." Jan reports that not only does she still teach that woman's child, but the mother has taken up piano lessons, too. Her piano students now number 36. She finds it amazing that women as well as men condone cheating but cannot reconcile themselves to group sex.

George is a 41-year-old truck driver in New York City. He and his well-proportioned wife Terry live in a small suburban New York community. His income (see chart) was typical for his job. George and Terry had been swinging for about four years when he happened to meet the owner of another trucking company at J. S. Exchange, a Manhattan swingers' club. Terry later told George that this businessman's wife often complained that they could not attend swings very often because her husband had to work late nights. There was a great deal of theft at his loading platform. George solved both problems for the trucking-company owner and at the same time increased his own income. He now supervises the loading operations for his new friend. As one wry observer pointed out, "I guess you can't trust anybody that doesn't screw your wife."

If the Kinsey Report of 1948 were to be revised today, it clearly would include major changes in its findings involving group sex. Today millions of married American couples have become part of this sexual phenomenon. The 1948 Kinsey Report described group sex more as a male-oriented sexual activity. Kinsey said,

"Most males who have participated in sexual activities in groups have found the opportunity to do so with prostitutes."

In major urban areas this is still true. There also is a sharp contrast in the attitudes of married male swingers who participate in group sex without their wives. Most suburban males interviewed along with their wives showed a greater concern for adding excitement and adventure to their married sexual relationship. But a group of businessmen in New York City who swung with prostitutes focused more on their personal accomplishments with a more crude verbalization.

Lew, a 41-year-old New York City textile manufacturer's representative who hired prostitutes for his business clients described his pitch this way:

"I say to these guys, listen, you pick up women all day long, you get these fifty-year-olds who love you. You waste your time and money in bars. Join us in our apartment for a real ball. Every Thursday night we bang our brains out —we can't even get a hard-on until the next week."

What Lew doesn't tell his customer is that when he joins the sex party he can expect Lew to stand over the bed with a pen and order pad in hand. Lew does not consider himself a pimp; rather, he is a businessman who has brought fun and games to his clients and at the same time profits to his business (see chart).

To keep his outside sales expenses to a minimum, Lew boasts that he is able to persuade some married women whose husbands "wouldn't think of swinging" to join his exclusive business arrangement without charging a prostitute's fee. Lew calls it his speech number 417. The following is Lew's account of his successful sales pitch:

"I had been fucking this gal Sandra from New Jersey, and I invited her up to the apartment. I didn't tell her it was our regular Thursday night swing, and when she saw the wall-to-wall sex, she got turned off and wanted to go home. That's when I took her into my 'office'—it's adjacent to the refrigerator in the kitchen. Besides, it was the only place in the apartment where there wasn't sex going on. Anyway, the speech is very simple. It's one that I have used successfully with at least a dozen broads who I personally have turned on to swinging. I say, 'Look, you're here, you came here on your own free volition. I'm going to tell you where it's at. We are a sociable group who engage in free sex. If you feel that you would like to have this with us, you are welcome to join us. But we don't jump on you. We don't attack or assault you. You are free to leave—the door swings both ways.' I give them their free choice. I continue along that vein where I make them feel that it is their option. I'm not forcing them to do a damn thing. More times than not they say that they will stay and at least try it out of curiosity. They may not come back a second time, but the majority stay for a swing that one time. The added incentive, of course, is that at least six or seven other gals are at that very moment swinging in the living room. Sandra was a classic case of someone who had not swung before. To make a long story short, she agreed to try it. By the time the night was over, she had been with all nine guys once—and one of the guys a second time. (For the first time in her life Sandra also had a sexual experience with one of the other gals.) She claims she had her first real orgasm."

Sandra became a regular member of Lew's swing-for-profit organization.

Sally Corwin lay in bed as she had done many nights after one of her "talkathons" with her husband Bud. But this time she knew she had to reach a final decision. Although married 17 years and fully satisfied with their sex life, both Bud and Sally realized that "something" was missing. Bud had decided that group sex would be the answer. Though Sally rejected the idea many times over the years since Bud originally brought the subject up, she had fantasized increasingly about sleeping with other men. Bud insisted that swinging would increase their passion together. Though she wasn't positive that swinging was the answer, she finally came to the realization that if she didn't give in and agree to swinging, Bud would have clandestine affairs with other women. The thought of that frightened her. She knew if that happened she would have to sue for divorce and would eventually be sleeping with other men, anyway.

"But group sex would not be cheating . . . would not be adultery . . . this would be mutual partner swapping," Bud argued. He repeatedly promised her they would give it up if she didn't like it. He was sure this was for them. Finally Sally slept, knowing that in the morning she would tell Bud she would go along with swinging.

Housewives in their thirties and forties are no different than their "sisters" in their early twenties when it comes to thinking of sex. Many older women want to "break out" of their puritanical past. They want to share in the sexual revolution. Before committing themselves to swinging, they ask themselves a number of questions: Can I satisfy another man? Is it really different with another man? Is it possible that I could fall in love with a swinger? What about precautions regarding pregnancy? What about the possibility of venereal disease? What if a man asks me to do something sexually that I've never done before? Will I do it? Will he be turned off if I don't? Will my husband really love me more seeing me have intercourse with another man? How will I feel knowing he is making love to another woman? Can we still maintain a relationship with "straight" friends?

The order of importance of these questions appears to be as varied as the women themselves. In the research for this chapter, we met and interviewed scores of swinging couples from Boston to New Jersey suburbs, to New York City swing clubs, to modern couples in California, home of the original swap revolution. For the purpose of our research we conducted a survey primarily among married couples. The above questions came from the wives themselves when we asked them their greatest concerns in making their decision to swing.

Can I satisfy another man?

This question was one that the authors found quite prevalent among women all over the country before they finally committed themselves to swinging. Surprisingly, no matter what their age, their hesitation was momentary. "I am a woman. Though something is missing I *KNOW* my husband can be satisfied—why not another man?" Joe, in suburban Chicago, whose wife is extremely attractive, said: "How personable is this woman? How is her personality? I think every woman feels hesitation for that reason. Dee had that hang-up when we got into it. She felt that she wouldn't turn men on. I know she is very attractive, but I think any woman, be she the most attractive or unattractive, has this feeling within herself. I've talked to other women, and they all seem to feel that way in the beginning." Dee, nodding all the while her husband was talking, said: "I've had two operations and have scars on my body that bother me." Before she could go on, Ben, a man she has swung with many times, said, "You know something? We've swung and I've never noticed any scars on your body." They all laughed. Dee went on. "We were married nineteen years, and though we are in love, we felt that there should be more to it than just a few kisses and going to bed with each other. I think it should be a very exciting feeling at all times, and I felt that I was beginning to miss this in my marriage. Maybe when the children were younger and I didn't have the time to concentrate on going to bed, even though we enjoyed it, I was not feeling womanly. I wanted to feel really very, very wanted as far as sex. I wanted my husband to want me like a different woman."

Is it really different with another man?

Once committed, women have said that the first time was exciting even though some tenseness was involved. But all experiences weren't as thrilling as those in fictional love stories. The variety of men and their techniques make swinging so exciting it is anticipated with the same intensity as avid bridge players about to sit down for a masters-points tournament.

Is it possible to fall in love with a swinger?

This has happened, but in rare cases. The general attitude of swingers is that their marriage is secure. They love each other totally, but they want an added extra that swinging with other couples will give them.

What about precautions regarding pregnancy?

Since the sixties and the widespread use of the birth-control pill, this has been of little concern. Women who are not on the pill may wear a "coil." Younger swingers who intend to have children are extremely cautious in their birth control while swinging. Vasectomies are becoming more popular, even to the extent that there is a club in Long Island that will not accept members unless the men show their final-examination certificate after their operation.

What if a man asks me to do something sexually that I've never done before? Will I do it? Will he be turned off if I don't?

Ben typified most men by saying: "If a woman has a particular sexual hang-up and her partner indicates he wants to do a certain thing which she doesn't want to do, she says, 'No thanks, I'd rather not,' and it's readily accepted." No woman should feel that she must perform a certain act to satisfy a swinging partner. If the act is one she had thought of doing with her husband but had never done, she may acquiesce. If it is an act she would rather not do and her partner insists, which isn't common, she can tell him that she has decided not to swing. She and her husband will make sure that they do not commit themselves to that particular couple in the future.

Will my husband love me more seeing me have intercourse with another man? How will I feel knowing he is making love to another woman?

Ted, a Bostonian, speaks for many men. "I enjoy swinging openly. Barbara and I look at each other. We kiss. A girl may be fellating me but Barbara can reach over and touch me, rub my arm. I'll play with her breasts. I tell you that with such honesty, well, there can't be more honesty in a marriage than right there at that particular time."

What about the possibility of venereal disease?

In San Francisco, Bob answered. "There is a fear in the back of your mind. But I have found that with the majority of swingers, they are very, very clean—ultra-clean. They are very conscious about their health and about their cleanliness. I try to avoid being with a girl that's single, and Sandy tries to avoid being with a single guy. Sometimes we may go to a party where a married man will bring a single chick. I try to stay away from those people. We like being with married people. There is always a chance, but with married couples it is limited. We know a couple who contracted VD and immediately called all the friends they had swung with the past two weeks and said, 'Look, we've got it, you better get yourselves checked.' But this is quite rare, especially among married swingers."

Can we still maintain a relationship with "straight" friends?

Yes. Though swingers all over the country prefer their swinging friends, they still have social evenings with straight friends. Most swingers feel that their sexual life is their own private life and don't feel the need to inform all their friends about it. Some couples swing two or three times a month and other couples may swing two or three times a week, depending on their circle of friends.

A Swinging New Year's Party

New Year's Eve 1971–72 was to be a special one for Harvey and Linda. After thinking about swinging for more than three years, they had been swinging for the previous six months and now were going to host their first swing party. They wanted it just right. Ed and Fran, who had been swingers for a number of years, helped them plan it. Arrangements were made with Harvey's mother to take the children for the weekend. Linda's artistic schooling was put to good use when she designed special invitations to 15 couples, all people who had been with each other at one time or another and who got along well socially.

Harvey and Linda's home is a four-bedroom colonial.

The day of the party, all the beds were taken apart with the frames resting against the walls. The mattresses and box springs were separated and laid out side by side in each room. A sign downstairs pointed toward the bedrooms: MEDITATION ROOMS—THIS WAY. Extra towels were supplied in the two upstairs bathrooms as well as in the half bath downstairs.

There were house rules; most important was that no one bring marijuana. The second rule was that swinging did not start until after midnight. "After all, husbands and wives should be together at the stroke of midnight." There was a third rule. No swinging in the living room. "This was not an orgy, and the bedrooms were the only rooms to be used."

As to attire, "casual" was the order of the evening. Some women wore pants suits, some wore minidresses, and one woman wore a granny dress buttoned up to her neck. During the course of the evening men and women walked around in the nude or in their underclothes. Some women wore just a man's shirt.

Most men averaged sexual relations about three to five times during the night. However, some of these may have been extended. One couple were upstairs for three hours.

In reminiscing about the party, Harvey recalled some of the pleasant memories. What excited him most was the variety of sex partners. "There were three types of gals at the party," he said with a slight grin. "There's the hummer, the moaner, and the screamer." Glancing at his wife he said, "Linda is a hummer. She sort of makes love with a rhythmic sigh, like HmmmmmmmMMmmmmmmMM." Linda chuckled at Harvey's impersonation. "Next comes the moaner who thinks every thrust is going to split her open, but she loves it. Finally there is the screamer." Again glancing at Linda, Harvey said, "You know who I mean. Fran. When she's turned on all you have to do is touch her and she lets loose with a screech that could wake the neighborhood. All but one of the guys knew Fran was a screamer, and he just so happened to be the first one to have her New Year's Eve. Just as he was about to get laid, Fran let out such a screech that three guys lost their hard-ons."

An interesting aspect of a swinger's party is that it actually costs less than a straight party. Considerably less liquor and food is consumed since they have something much more enticing to take up their time. Harvey and Linda's party was such a success that nine of the fifteen couples stayed until ten o'clock in the morning and ended the party with a full breakfast. After a nap of a few hours at their respective homes, four couples came back to help put the beds back in order and clean the house. By the time the children came home, the house was spotless.

Group-Sex Swing Kits

While a great deal of money has been made from the swingers movement through swingers magazines, swingers clubs, swingers lodges, etc., there appears to be one potential financial enterprise involving swingers that has not been explored commercially. When it was brought to the authors' attention that most swinging couples utilize what they call a "swingers kit," one group-sex club operator wondered whether there was a potential profit to be made by packaging such a kit. These kits contain beauty and health aids, but there are exceptions. One such kit was displayed for the authors at a swing party with the following description by its owner—who is a very active member of a New York City swingers club:

"As you can see, I utilize a regular men's toilet-article case. Here is the normal toothbrush and toothpaste, a large bottle of Brut cologne and a bottle of Brut 33 Fabergé deodorant, comb, and a few items you don't normally find in a traveling salesman's overnight bag. This is a vibrator shaped like a penis. It's operated with two flashlight batteries, and most of the women love it. Naturally I have a small jar of Vaseline for tight situations, and this is a bottle of passion oil—its called Reward and has a nice odor. I put a very small amount on a woman's breasts or vagina and blow on it. It gives them a very warm feeling and turns a lot of women on. You can't buy it in a corner drugstore, but it is available from advertisements in the swingers magazines. I still have a few more items like this lubricated Trojan condom in case a girl who didn't expect to swing changes her mind but doesn't have a coil or didn't bring along her diaphragm or foam."

He explained that both he and his wife carry ordinary health and beauty aids to a swing and will utilize these items after each sexual relationship. "After all," he said, "you want to be ready for the next swing, and personal hygiene is a big part of it." His wife agreed. "After a bedroom swing we usually come out and socialize for a while and you don't want to look bad—you want to look presentable for the next man." Her swing kit included the following: feminine hygiene deodorant spray, underarm deodorant, mascara, eye shadow, blush, foundation, curlers, Helena Rubinstein Skin Dew, eye make-up, lipstick, toothbrush, a miniature sewing kit, Nivea skin cream (in case of irritation), and two different perfumes—Styx and a very sexy French perfume called Parfum de Toilette Je Reviens (I Return).

Several swingers interviewed said that they hoped someone would invent a small disposable douche, something like a fleet enema, a one-time shot that could be thrown away after a single use.

During our research of one suburban group-sex club we were able to count the number of participants by tallying the number of leather toilet-article kits lined up on the fireplace mantle at the hosts' home.

Best Friends

Published estimates on the extent of group sex in the United States range from 500,000 to 5 million. It seems to us that it is an impossible task to come up with any definitive figures. But there is one phase of the group-sex phenomenon that apparently is more common than any other discussed thus far. That is, couple swapping, limited to "best friends."

Mike and Marlene and Ray and Estelle had been the best of friends for five years. They spent most of their time together and were rarely invited out separately. They even spent vacations with each other. Their children referred to them as "aunt" and "uncle." Mike and Ray had talked with each other about swinging clubs. Both men assured one another that their love for their wives was as great as the day they married, but both felt the desire and need of "something sexually different." Yet neither would admit how great that desire really was.

Unknown to them, Marlene and Estelle had, as many women do, discussed various aspects of their sexual lives with each other. Often, couched with carefully selected clichés, the women would agree that their sex life was good, but they felt it was boring at times—too repetitive.

One summer evening they were together for a barbecue and a swim in Ray and Estelle's pool. The children were already asleep, and they were relaxing with cocktails when Mike brought up the subject of swinging. Marlene and Estelle said that they would never consider it. Mike asked, "What about swapping?" For a few moments, they couldn't look one another in the eye. But apparently Mike knew the mood was right. He continued to lead a discussion. "It seems to be such a natural experience for us to share," he said. "We have been the best of friends, and we trust one another implicitly." Putting his arms around Estelle, he continued, "This would be another example of our closeness."

It was a warm evening. Ray turned off the swimming-pool floodlights and invited Marlene into the pool. Mike and Estelle followed without a word. Mike made the first move. He caressed Estelle's breasts under the water and slowly removed the top of her two-piece bathing suit. He slid out of his trunks and the two embraced tightly. Ray and Marlene, at the other end of the dark pool, were kissing and petting passionately. With the swirling warm water splashing against her nude body, Marlene whispered across the pool to her husband and her best friend, "Let's go in the house." She didn't know whether they would think she didn't like what was going on, so she quickly added, "To the bedroom." Mike's knees began to shake. Estelle had a funny feeling in her stomach.

Ray and Marlene took the master bedroom, Mike and Estelle, the den. The long-time friendship, the feeling that all of this was so natural, led to a most gratifying sexual relationship that began that night.

Sometimes being away from home is the impetus to establishing a new relationship between best friends. This was the case with Ann and Bob and Ted and Pat. The best of friends for over six years, they too, like Mike and Marlene, Ray and Estelle, spent most of their time together, including vacations. One year they decided that they would like to vacation at Cape Cod, Massachusetts, instead of Lake George, New York, as they usually did. After leaving their children with babysitters for the weekend, they drove the five hours to Cape Cod. Since it was mid-March, they felt they wouldn't need to make reservations in a motel. They spent the day looking over various cottages and finally found the perfect summer home. Then they drove around for another two hours trying to find a mantic, old-fashioned inn and enjoyed their dinner in front of a blazing fireplace.

Later they relaxed with after-dinner cocktails in Ann and Bob's room. It was a typical motel room, two beds, a night table, bureau with TV, and one chair. When Bob had to go out to his car for a bag, he returned to find that Ted was relaxing on one bed and Pat on the other. Ann was sitting on the one chair. Bob sat down on Pat's bed. Ann, following his example, sat down on Ted's bed. It seemed natural to just sit back and relax and watch TV together.

Although the four of them had never discussed swapping, Bob and Ann had wondered what it would be like. However, the subject never came up openly when the four of them were together. Apparently Ted and Pat must have discussed the subject, too, because soon Ted's fingers were lightly stroking Ann's arm. Bob was reluctant to make any move toward Pat, but when he glanced at Ted and Ann and saw that Ann wasn't objecting, he decided that he, too, would make a move with Pat. Just then Pat's leg moved slightly until it touched Bob's. He started to caress her breasts. It didn't take long for the four of them to realize that their friendship could extend to an even deeper relationship. That was the night their mate swapping began.

At the time the authors interviewed them, the two couples were quite sure that they would never join a club with strangers and were quite happy with their relationship limited to mate swapping with their "best friends."

Swingers Clubs and Magazines—How Swingers Meet

Businessmen know that if they want to buy, sell, or swap merchandise they must advertise their wares. The same is true for swingers who want to find "like-minded" couples to join with them in their sexual adventures. It would be unlikely to find such an advertisement in the *New York Times*, although there are some regular daily newspapers across the country that have unknowingly accepted swingers classified advertisements for the Personal columns.

One such announcement was found in a suburban New Jersey newspaper that announced a weekly swingers club. It was worded:

MODERN COUPLES—COME SWING WITH "OUR FRIENDS"
FOR INFORMATION CALL — —— OR — ——.

The authors checked with the two couples who placed this advertisement, listing their home telephone numbers, and learned that they had just started a couples swing club. They told us that the response was overwhelming, and 36 couples paid $5 per couple to attend their opening Friday-night swing-club gathering. However, this type of publicity is rare.

The most common advertising is found in the specialized swingers magazines such as *Select*. *Select* boasts that it is the largest swingers contact magazine with nationwide listings. A recent issue of the Camden, New Jersey, publication contained 4,100 personal ads of men, women, and couples who sought to meet other swingers. The magazine sells for $3 and includes hundreds of photographs, mostly of nude women. The listings are by states, with New York and New Jersey accounting for most of the ads. This is not necessarily an indication of the geographical extent of swinging. West Coast publications show a greater number of Californians participating in the swinging scene. The specific profits of magazines such as *Select* are unavailable. However, the following figures give an idea of the potential profits:

Subscription cost—per issue $3.00
Personal ad rate @ 10¢ per word—
  per issue—average words 35 .... 3.50
Charge for forwarding replies $1.08
  (including postage) 5 average no. replies 5.40

For the purpose of estimating gross income, if the 4,100 advertisers to *Select* purchased an issue and responded with an average of five replies, that would total $48,790. If only a like number purchased the magazine and responded to an average of five ads, without personally advertising themselves, that would increase the gross income of *Select* magazine by another $34,440. These figures are probably quite conservative. A total gross income from the magazine for one issue of 8,200 copies amounts to $83,230.

The wording of advertisements is as varied as the desires of those advertising. Here is an example of a typical ad placed by a California couple:

SPLISH-SPLASH . . . Make waves and each other on our waterbed. Young Orange Co. couple seeks other young upright men and wayward ladies whose schooling took them beyond high school. French and ancient Gr. cul. Photo appreciated.

This ad was accompanied by a code number. Respondents enclose their replies in sealed envelopes, place them in covering envelopes, and mail them to *Select* magazine with the amount payable for the replies. In turn, the magazine forwards them to the California couple within 24 hours.

The publishers of *Select* magazine know they have a good thing going for them. In a recent issue they advertised *Select* club franchises available. They also conduct regular *Select* socials, that is, regular weekend sex retreats

in major cities around the country. In a given 30-day period such Select socials were held in Boston, Cleveland,
and Philadelphia. Reservations had to be accompanied by
a $25 fee per couple. That fee included social-club admis-
sion, hot buffet dinner, live music, prizes, and souvenirs.
As many as 100 couples have attended these gatherings.

While there are many legitimate swingers magazines
available, there are dozens of phony publications sold at
underground newsstands such as in the Times Square
area of New York City. These range in price from $3 to
$5 and are primarily sold for their pornographic value.
Most of the ads in these publications include pictures of
studio models trying to sell their wares. One such so-
called swingers magazine published in New York City
with hundreds of advertisements is believed to have at
least a 70 percent no-reply rate.

The other method of meeting swingers is through the
growing number of swingers clubs. In New York City the
authors were able to locate a half-dozen such clubs that
usually operated on Friday nights. They also promote vacation weekend activities including a swingers nudist-
camp gathering in the summer or a swingers winter-won-
derland weekend in the Catskills of New York.

One New York City club called the Inner-Sanctum promotes its Friday night activities with parties and contests.
For example, Inner-Sanctum had a "cleavage generation"
party and contest with the ten best cleavage contestants
winning free champagne. The following week the same
club conducted a micro-mini competition. The ten brief-
est micro-mini skirts brought awards of champagne.

New York City club membership fees average $15 per
couple. That fee entitles the couple to admission at the
usual Friday night pub bashes. The clubs usually operate
in existing bars and regular dinner clubs in private rooms
rented for the occasion. They, in turn, operate their own
bars for big profits, and some swingers who have fled the

New York City scene say they don't like the operators of some of these clubs always pushing watered-down drinks at above-average costs. Many suburban couples have fled the city scene, too, because of the overcrowded atmosphere. They complain that it is just not congenial enough for their sexual appetites. In its promotional brochure the J. S. Exchange Club in New York City boasts that it is the most successful couples-only swingers club. It goes on to state:

> Today, we are over 800 couples and our weekly socials are highly successful, drawing between 150–200 people each and every week. Always maintaining a friendly house party atmosphere. With our goals being, honest friendship, understanding of our fellow man, good cheer coupled with a sincere responsibility to others. Our rules are brief, to the point, self-explanatory, and are an extension of every day living. Good taste implies that everyone will follow the three C's (1) COUPLES (2) COURTESY (3) CHARACTER.

SWINGER'S CAREER CHART

Occupation	Annual income before swinging	Annual income after involvement	Explanation
Owner, secretarial service	$31,500	$ 39,000	Met numerous doctors and lawyers in married swinging clubs who began utilizing his firm's services.
Textile-manufacturer representative	26,000	35,000	A businessman who operated a weekly swinging orgy for clients. For those who didn't bring wives to participate he supplied prostitutes to be their swingers-party partners.
Truck driver	12,000	17,000	Took over loading-platform supervisor's job part-time—for owner of another trucking company. He often "swung" with owner and his wife.
Lawyer	48,000	58,000	Lawyers represent the largest single professional group among swingers. Often, business referrals are shared among swinger attorneys as well as new clients from trusting fellow swingers.

SWINGER'S CAREER CHART (Continued)

Occupation	Annual income before swinging	Annual income after involvement	Explanation
Car salesman	15,000	25,000	Social contacts made through swingers club became permanent customers. Sales led to promotion to sales manager.
Department-store chain vice-president	38,000	45,000	Already had position but solidified job by introducing firm's president to swinging. Was granted pay-raise request soon after, although two previous requests were refused.
Shoe buyer	18,000	23,000	Often brought his wife along on business trips. She persuaded firm-owner's wife to become a swinger.

19
(Bed) Room at the Top

"If you don't understand something about sex," writes Dr. Eric Berne, who was one of the most eminent psychiatrists in America, "don't say it's awful or mysterious. Look it up in Freud."

It is not possible to put all the inhabitants of the executive suite on the Freudian couch *en masse*, but the arts of psychiatry, social work, psychology, and psychotherapy surely have something to say about the people who mix business and pleasure with an eye toward profit. So, to get some professional insight into the goings-on in the bedroom at the top, the authors consulted Martin A. Adler, a certified psychotherapist, social worker, and marriage counselor. He is executive director of the Community Center for Mental Health in Bergen County, New Jersey. Dr. Adler also has his own private practice where he consults with individuals and couples about their sexual problems at the Hillcrest Medical Center, Spring Valley, New York.

A pleasant man with graying brown hair curling stylishly over the collar, Adler consults in a pleasant office surrounded by a wide variety of books of both a general and a medical nature. He sees sex as just another facet of doing business. That corporations and corporate executives traffic in sex does not surprise him nor interest him in any unusual way. "Rather," he says, "it is the motivations and drives of the individuals themselves that should be of interest to us."

On that basis Adler reviewed cases presented in this book, analyzing them for the psychological motivations of those individuals. "That these persons have made a business of their sexuality is merely a symptom of their problems—and that's what they are—which subconsciously gnaw at them," he says, gesturing with his hands and puffing at a pipe he clenched between his teeth throughout his discussion of the occupants of the executive suite.

AUTHORS: The story of K, the very successful executive secretary, gave every indication that her entire motivation was to get to the top. Being an ordinary secretary was not enough. She had to be an executive secretary.

ADLER: It is almost as if this very bright girl is trying to fulfill her father's promise of success which he never achieved. She will be successful whereas he was not. The financial goal is a side goal. She is trying to achieve her father's success by relating to successful men. Basically, most prostitutes, most women who are actively involved in this kind of sexual exchange, tend to be schizoid people who can only effect a physical communication and not an emotional one. When they say they are seeking love, they are talking truth but not in the sense of love as they openly say it but love they never really received. They are trying to fill the emptiness they came from. They desperately want love, but they can accept it only in a physical way. The women that I've had contact with can talk very freely and intimately about their sexual activity on a money-exchange basis. They think money is a way of achieving a goal. They talk about a financial goal. But what they are really talking about is their being a successful person, and a successful person is one who will receive what was never receivable before. The father in K's case is talking about being successful; someday it will happen. The mother is domineering and ridiculing the father. A girl in this environment could very easily begin to vow, "I will be successful, like my father will be successful, and I will fulfill my father's promise. I will do it by being with successful men." The girl needs to be two things: what her father would have liked to be and the successful daughter of her mother. She becomes "my daughter the prostitute," and she receives parental attention. Girls like this become quite suicidal in their late twenties because they are receiving only a transferrable love. It is transferred to them during the act and then is transferred when the act is over. All a girl is left with is a few dollars. A girl like this is driven to find other contacts.

AUTHORS: You equate the successful woman who uses sex to get ahead with the prostitute.

ADLER: They are prostitutes.

AUTHORS: Suicide is a likely end for a prostitute?

ADLER: After a period of years, girls like this often kill themselves. Statistically, prostitutes and call girls have a high suicide rate. They have what we sometimes call an hysterical character disorder. They act out in this way while desperately searching for something. They say they want money or success, but they don't achieve what they really want, which is love. They recognize that they are empty. Many of them go on drugs. Many of them are alcoholics. And at some sober point in their life, recognizing their complete emptiness, they kill themselves.

AUTHORS: What kills them? Lack of love? A realization that success is not what they were looking for?

ADLER: There is a strong masochistic element in this. Though they talk about success and say this is the culture of our time, it is not culture that drives us. Culture is what we use as an adaptation of our inner need. It is the inner

AUTHORS: Many executives do participate even in group sex. These are the men who accept the favors of the so-called referral agencies.

ADLER: It is risky to generalize, but generalize we will. There are times when people use the words "swinger" and "masculinity" as synonymous. Many men who regard themselves as swingers use this to portray themselves the way men used to portray themselves as Don Juans. You can get very Freudian with people like this. If as a young-ster a businessman had a father who was in business and his mother was having affairs of her own, this young man would determine that this is the way life is. Every child senses and seeks desperately to determine, "What do my parents really want of me? What do they expect? What is the way to reach Mom and Dad?" At an early age they do not see or understand amoral activity. "What must I now do?" What is the parent interested in? It's quite possible that Ernie or men like him see that their mother is sexu-ally involved while father is involved in his business. You could make a case for saying that Ernie's sexual activities are a model of what his parents were doing. He is proving something to both of them.

AUTHORS: One man described previously went around while his clients were having sexual intercourse and made them sign up then and there for orders. What about a guy like that?

ADLER: When he says to that client that it's time to sign up for a $5,000 order, he is demonstrating his business abilities by getting the order, and also exhibiting peculiar behavior. When he says, "Here is the order" and that this is really a business practice, doesn't he see his own voyeuristic pathology here? Or if he does see it why doesn't he want to do anything about it?

AUTHORS: How about the businessman who engages in group sex?

ADLER: Frequently many of these men can become very

sexually active with strangers but when it comes to being a sexually mature and successful person with their own wives, they may lack. One damned good way of not showing this lack is to blame the lack of sexual contact at home with the wife on the group-sex activity. There are plenty of excuses. How sexually active were these men you interviewed with their own wives?

AUTHORS: Many don't have that much activity with their wives.

ADLER: I would wonder how much homosexuality is involved in these group activities by these men. I would wonder whether there is a degree of homosexuality implied in some of these group-sex activities.

AUTHORS: There was a great amount among the women. Among the men we did not notice any homosexuality in the groups that we observed.

ADLER: Homosexuality between women doesn't seem to have the same negative emotional impact as between men. Homosexuality may exist between two men without their being consciously aware of it or even touching one another. If they are involved sexually side-by-side each on a woman, there is a completely different feeling and atmosphere—sweat aroma and sexual atmosphere—in the act. If you are screwing a girl and another man is screwing another girl alongside of you, why do it next to one another? Why not do it in privacy unless you are getting something from this joint screwing side by side?

AUTHORS: There are two kinds of group sex. One is closed, that is, a couple in a room alone, but lots of rooms. The other is like the old-fashioned Roman orgy, everybody together, wall-to-wall mattresses. The latter is liked by those who regard themselves as exhibitionists or voyeurs.

ADLER: The reason that these people give for group sex is that they are sexual sophisticates, they are sexually free, and society prevents them from doing what they want, so they have set up their own organizations. At some point, I am sure, the question will come up that if they are that free and that sexually uninhibited, what other sexual expressions can we indulge in to test our freedom? If they have been involved in heterosexual activity, there is only one other kind of sexual activity left—homosexuality. I would expect that to be the next step. There has already been contact without the physical sexual contact. There has been voyeurism, and what is voyeurism? It is more than just observing what is going on. It is putting yourself in the place of what is going on. There is some similarity between group-sex activity and group therapy. Successful group therapy is where seven or eight people are expressing their repressed feelings. A couple may have had what they considered a fair sexual relationship before their involvement in group sex. I could see where after having released their feelings, they go home and feel better about sex and are able to relate better.

At no time did Adler make any moral judgments about the use of sex as a tool of business. While finding much material worthy of consideration by way of the personal attitudes, motives, and psychological drives of those who engaged in sexual activities as part of their daily business lives, the psychotherapist viewed sex in the executive suite as an "accepted business practice."

Our research has underscored the depths to which the practice has pervaded American business. "The business of America is business," said President Calvin Coolidge. Some years later, Wendel L. Wilkie added, "The glory of America is business."

The glorious business of America trades on flesh, using sex as "accepted business practice" whether as bribe or blackmail; in the corridors of power; in lunchtime assignations in Chicago, Boston, New York, Hollywood, Philadelphia, and in all the other cities from Maine to Hawaii; over drinks, in board meetings, through subterfuge, around the town, in the air, on the sea, around the corner, down the block, in hotels, motels, and apartments; in cars, on trains, in rest rooms, in elevators; at cocktail parties, in grand ballrooms, on lonely street corners, in crowded convention halls or empty saloons; on a couch, in a chair, or on a bed by those who get it, those who give it, and those who use it.

"Sex is a commodity," observed one of the business practitioners of the glorious business of America, "and if it were ever traded on the stock market, it would lead the list."

To a great extent sex has become a way for American business to avoid the one characteristic that made American industry so successful—the competition of the marketplace in which the goal was to make a better product more inexpensively than someone else and thereby make a quality product available to everyone. The sales representative who used to call on a prospective client with a persuasive discussion of why his company's products were superior now takes the prospective client to dinner on an expense account, flatters him, tells him funny stories, and generally entertains him—to the point of providing him with a girl. The business decision is made on the basis of who can sexually gratify the client not on the basis of which competing company best serves that man and *his* customers. Old-fashioned business competition has gone by the boards. Sex has been the cop-out.

And what of the people of the executive suite? If their companies have taken the easy way to avoid the rough and tumble of competition in the marketplace, have the decision-makers copped out, too? The answer is yes, but sex is only part of their story. It seems logical that people who have shortened their actual working hours from ten A.M. to noon and two P.M. to four P.M., with a morning coffee break and an afternoon coffee break, would ultimately bring sex into their business day. Sex is more fun than a long lunch, sweeter than a Danish roll. Out of the same boredom that has given rise to the minimal work day, those of the executive suite have turned to sex as another way to eliminate boredom.

Here, then, are people who are bored in a business community of national scope that is afraid of competition. Personally and for business reasons they turn to man's oldest diversion. The frantic hope is that sex will wipe out the boredom and eliminate the need for honest competition.

Because we believe this to be true, we conclude that the sexual aspects of American business reflect a phenomenon noted by many sociologists and psychologists in analyzing life in America in the last half of the 20th century—ennui, boredom, purposelessness. "What's it all about?" Americans ask themselves, whether they be teenagers dropping out of school, young men rebelling against the American ideal of obtaining a college education and a good job, dissenters from the Puritan work ethic, groups of young adults taking up communal farming, or accomplished executives abandoning careers and settling for menial work that will leave them time for what they would really like to do.

The businessman who hires prostitutes to persuade customers to do business with him chooses the easy way and turns away from the hard competition that was the hallmark of businessmen in other eras. He is basically the same as the corporations, farmers, and labor unions that turn to the government for protective laws to make it easier for them to compete. The rule of American business has often been, "How can we find an easier way to do this?" For some the answer is protective tariffs or government subsidies. For others it has been through the device of providing sexual enticement where good business practices might be insufficient.

And what is to be said of the potential customer who chooses to do business with someone solely, or largely, on the basis of the fact that he is serviced sexually? At what point does his business, his service, or his product suffer because he has become more interested in taking care of himself than his own customers? The motto of these businessmen has become, "What have you done for me lately?"

Sex in the executive suite is just another symptom of the malaise of the spirit that seems to have become evident in almost every aspect of life in the United States, but because it can have a negative effect, the implications for the state of American business are serious. A decline in the vigor of American business necessarily means a decline in the vigor of America. If it is true as Calvin Coolidge observed that the business of America is business, then serious questions about the state of American business must be raised when one of the men in this book observed, "Sex is the necessary lubricant of business."

20
Appendix I.
A Guide to
Executive Sex-cess

Paraphrasing Ogden Nash, it is safe to say with impunity that the world of business is a place of opportunity. The question the executive will ask is, "Should I?" The question *should be*, "Why shouldn't I?"

There is no reason an executive shouldn't, except one —getting caught at it.

By adopting the motto of the Boy Scouts, any average executive may readily eliminate the prospect of getting caught at it. The following guide should be of help to even the wariest of business executives who feel that the time is ripe for a little swinging. This Guide to Executive Sex-cess is arranged in a simple, easy-to-follow question-and-answer style for ease of understanding and ready reference.

Business Sex-cess

1. Why should I indulge in sex during or as part of my business?
Answer: a. Everyone else is doing it.
b. It's fun.
c. It's relaxing.
d. It makes you a better person.
e. It saves the expense of psychoanalysis.
f. It's better than going to a baseball game.
g. It's nonfattening and helps you keep trim.
h. It can be profitable.
i. It brings in extra business.
j. It's the American way.
2. With whom should I engage in sex as part of business?
Answer: a. Your secretary.
b. The girls in the steno pool.
c. Secretaries of your business contacts.
d. In some cases, your business contacts.
e. Girls provided by your business contacts.
f. Girls in the hospitality rooms at conventions.
g. Airline stewardesses.
h. Your lawyer's secretary.
i. Your accountant's secretary.
j. Targets of opportunity.
3. With whom should I avoid sex as part of business?
Answer: a. Your boss's secretary.
b. Your boss's wife (in that order!).
4. When should I engage in sex as part of business?
Answer: a. Now.
b. During coffee breaks.
c. On vacations (without your family along).
d. During the lunch hour.
e. Tuesdays.
f. During the cocktail hour.

g. During meetings (if the whole office is into group sex).

h. In rented cars on short trips.

i. When giving dictation.

j. On the long-distance telephone.

5. Where should I do it?

Answer: a. In your office.

b. In her office.

c. In the board of directors conference room when conferences are not being held (unless the board is into group sex).

d. In the boss' office when he is out of town.

e. In a motel.

f. At her place.

g. In a hotel.

h. In a car.

i. In a weekend ski lodge or beach house.

j. In elevators between floors during blackouts.

k. In the supply closet.

6. How do I get the money I may need?

Answer: a. Petty cash.

b. Arrange to have bonuses paid in separate checks.

c. Open a savings account.

d. Open a credit-card account in your name only and have all bills mailed to your office.

e. Let her pay.

f. Put it on a company credit card.

g. Use your lunch money.

h. Charge it to business expenses.

Note: In cases where the sex is being provided by a client you need not pay; cultivate this kind of arrangement.

7. How do I avoid getting caught?

Answer: See below, "Give-aways."

8. Should I patronize call girls?

Answer: a. If someone else is paying.
          b. If your tastes run to the exotic.
          c. If you are in a hurry.
          d. If you are too shy to ask someone you know.
WARNING: Patronizing streetwalkers or bar girls is fraught with the dangers of arrest, disease, blackmail, poor taste, slim pickings, and loss of social stature. You may also be mugged and have a hard time explaining that to your wife.
9. Should I have an affair?
Answer: Yes, but remember that the cost of keeping two women (mistress and wife) is twice the cost of keeping one.

The Affair

A married man is well prepared to have an affair. He has already made adjustments to keeping a woman. He is housebroken, so to speak. Remember that an affair *is* an affair and not a substitute for the marriage you already have. The affair should never reach the point where it jeopardizes everything you have going for you in the marriage—mortgage, car payments, bills for your kids' education, dental bills, doctor and hospital expenses, in-laws, installment payments, and taxes. Committing oneself to an affair is not, remember, committing oneself to an endless, open-ended arrangement. This should be the understanding at the outset. Because honesty is always the best policy, be honest with the woman who will be sharing this affair. Tell her it is *not* forever. If she coyly announces, "Well, we'll just see what develops," do not proceed. When the terms are agreed, the affair may begin but always with certain precautions:
    1. Do not let her quit her job. Stress upon her that you and she are equals in this arrangement. Do not hesitate to let her pick up the check occasionally.

2. Discourage letter and card writing by her to you. Too many wives of executives have cleaned out inside pockets or briefcases while doing their wifely thing.

3. Wallet pictures of your mistress are *verboten*.

4. Utilize code names in your address book. Female names become male names: example, Alice is Al, Roberta is Rob. (If her name is Zelda, you have problems.)

5. Never list right phone numbers. Reverse the order of digits. Imagine your wife calling an uncoded number in your book to ask for Al and having Alice answer that no one named Al lives there but her name is Alice and may she be of help?

6. Codify addresses, also.

7. Keep a large supply of clean handkerchiefs at your office to avoid the lipstick-on-the-handkerchief trap.

8. Take taxis to your rendezvous places. This eliminates the need to explain parking tickets received at strange addresses.

9. Get in the habit of using strong colognes. They hide the lingering aroma of your girl friend's perfume and eliminate the need to drive home with the windows open to air out the car.

10. If using hotels for your assignations, book them through the office at special "business meeting" rates available at most hotels.

11. When you want only an afternoon quickie, use finesse. Don't tell her it's just a fast bang. Arrange to have your office call you and urgently request your return.

12. Never leave your son alone in the office. He snoops at home, why shouldn't he snoop at the office? If your mistress happens to be your secretary and very young, it is doubly important to keep your son out of the office. You give him enough already.

13. Never call her from your home. Wives check phone bills.

14. When using a regular poker game with the boys as

an excuse for being out at night, be sure to tell your wife that one of the inflexible rules of the game is that no player can be called away to take a phone call from a wife. Establish a reputation as a heavy loser. This will account for funds spent on the other woman.

15. Do not invite the other woman to your son's bar mitzvah, your daughter's wedding, or your grandson's christening. She will, of course, attend your funeral, but what do you care?

16. Do not use bowling as an excuse for a night out. You have to lug the bowling ball everywhere you go.

With these rules firmly in mind as you make your commitment to have an affair, give very careful thought to with whom you will share this adventure. You may consider your secretary, but this is an undertaking fraught with booby traps. Some days you just won't want to see your mistress, so why have her just outside your office? Secretaries are the first people suspected by wives. When it comes time to end the affair (see special section on this below), you will also have to fire your secretary. This might seem an easy thing, but it is far easier to find a good mistress than it is a good secretary.

Where to find a candidate? A few examples: local Democratic clubs and local Republican clubs (in that order), church services and socials, parks where you walk your dog or take your children to fly kites, grocery shopping (volunteer to do this for your wife but do not take her along), your local fair-housing association or other liberal organizations, the reading room of the library (exclude the Christian Science Reading Room), and in bookstores.

Do not seek companionship at these places: the local gin mill, service stations, weight-watchers meetings, barbershops (unless they are unisex), the drugstore, doctor's office, dentist's office, Iwo Jima, Antarctica, West Point, and Dubuque, Iowa.

Do not seek the companionship of women who are fond of: John Wayne movies, suits, scented cigarettes, boots, knitting, telephoning, expensive jewelry, sports cars, blue-chip stocks, Swiss bank accounts, cheese fondue, hairnets, other women, and long fingernails with which to leave inexplicable scratches down your back.

This brings us to technique.

Technique

1. Where? See No. 5 above, *Business Sex-cess.*

2. When? See No. 4 above, *Business Sex-cess.*

3. Be prepared. Discuss with your partner the precautions to be taken and insist that she take them. The pill, IUD, etc., are infinitely safer and more pleasurable for you. Tell her that you have moral, political, social, and aesthetic objections to condoms in any form.

4. Be natural. An affair is a situation calling for the abandonment of all hang-ups. Indulge your fantasies. Make them fact. Use words as well as you use your body. Following is a partial list of things to say: (You are a smart fellow and will be able to think of others.)

"You have pretty toes."

"I want to lick your fingers."

"I like you a lot."

"Where did you ever learn to do that?"

"You constantly amaze me."

"You scare me sometimes."

"Having an affair means never having to say you're sorry."

"Kiss me like that again, I think I might have missed something."

"Let's just do our thing."

"Sex is being free."

"Free me."

"Let me free you."

"We sure can communicate!"

"You are for real."

"Now I know what real beauty is."

5. Be careful. Certain things should never be said. Examples:

"I love you."

"My wife would never do that."

"I wish we could be together more often."

"I don't care about anything but us."

"You mean the whole world to me."

"I'd give you the world if I could." (She may settle for much less.)

"Divorce."

"Marriage."

6. Things to do with your hands: Pinch a toe, stroke the bridge of her nose with one fingertip, squeeze, stroke, pet, cup, fondle.

7. Things to do with your mouth: Kiss, lick, laugh, smile, pucker, suck, taste, and anything else that occurs to you.

8. Study an illustrated book of sexual techniques and positions and try them. Study the book *before,* not during. There may be a few positions you wish to avoid: standing on your head, chinning yourself, or other strenuous activities that you haven't done since basic training (and, then, not while you were screwing).

9. Get some stag films and watch them while engaging in foreplay. Suggest that she play follow the leader with the gal in the film by emulating what she does in the movie.

10. Make a tape recording of one of your encounters and play it back at your next session. Do not let this tape out of your possession and destroy it after you are finished with it. Avoid Polaroid pictures. They are durable and acceptable as evidence.

11. Choose music to enhance the mood. Do not be so cliché as to put on a recording of Ravel's *Bolero*. Try the *1812 Overture*. If you practice, you can reach a climax just as the cannons go off.

12. If you are into drugs, know which enhance sexuality and which dull it.

13. Make everything you do sensual, including undressing. Stripping should not be an interruption of the scene but part of it. Interweave the undressing with your foreplay. Why use fingers to loosen a garment when teeth can do it and at the same time provide affectionate love nips? Don't scratch yourself, even if you itch terribly. Avoid baggy drawers. Don't stop to fold your clothes and hang them up. *Abandon* them!

14. After, clean up. Get together a clean-up kit containing:

> strong cologne
> mouthwash or breath spray (wives can smell another woman on your breath just as surely as they can sniff out booze)
> wash-and-dry towelettes
> an extra pair of shoelaces
> an extra button (shirt) and small sewing kit
> spot remover
> comb
> handkerchief

Giveaways

It does not take a Sherlock Holmes to know a guy has been catting around if:

1. Matchbooks from lounges and clubs are found in pockets by wives who have never been to those establishments.

2. Bills from credit-card companies list places wives have never visited.

3. There is a girdle (not your wife's) in the glove compartment of the car.

4. Unusual increases in the auto-mileage gauge are noted when you have not been taking business trips. (Again, use cabs or other public transportation.)

5. Routines of day-to-day living suddenly change.

6. Health improves or takes a turn for the worse.

Ending It

There is no better way to end it than to say, "Good-bye." Anything else will prolong the agony and perhaps get you in deeper.

Ending it should have been part of the plan from the very beginning. From the very first lay you should also be laying the groundwork for the final farewell. This can be done very subtly. "I wish this could go on forever," you whisper into her ear as she lies cradled in your affectionate arms, "but. . . ." Or, "I don't know what I'm going to do without you." These are accepted as terms of endearment when spoken during the affairs but when said often enough register subconsciously as definite signs that this affair cannot go on always. It is never acceptable or even safe to break off the affair (as the Cole Porter lyric put it) with a good-bye, dear, and amen, and a hope that you'll meet now and then. Meeting now and then after it's over is OUT.

Be noble. "This has made a better person out of me."

Be grateful. "There is no way to repay the things you've given me and taught me."

Be philosophical. "What a bittersweet thing it is to see all this end. I knew it had to end this way. So did you. Let's remember how sweet it was and know that without the sadness of our parting there could never have been the lovely togetherness that preceded it."

Be firm. "It's over. We must accept that."

Golden Rule for Executive Sex-cess

DON'T PANIC. After all, what's the worst that can happen to you? Divorce, lose the kids, your Cadillac, your home, three-quarters of your income? Just think of the adventure you had and what a great lay that strange broad was.

Appendix II.
A Girl's Guide to
Executive Sex-cess

The first question to be answered by a gal who is considering obtaining dividends from her sexuality is whether she wants to be a pro or an amateur. There's something to be said for either choice. Pro, of course, means becoming a call girl. Getting laid *and* paid. Going into business. Amateur standing has its rewards, too: job security, job advancement, and all the little extras that go with being "the other woman." The disadvantages should be understood as well. As a pro you could get arrested. As an amateur your chances of finally marrying the guy you're playing around with are practically nil. Below, the authors outline effective, practical guides for both the pro and the amateur.

The Call Girl

1. Basic decisions:

a. Working alone. This is not recommended. To try to set up your own trade in clients probably means you'll be walking the streets. This causes colds, sore feet, arrests, venereal disease, threats from the tough competition. It can be exciting, and you could always write a book about life in a women's prison when you get out.

b. Working for a madam. The most effective way to get into "the life." Meeting madams is easy. Chances are one of the gals in your office or your apartment house is already working for one, so ask around. Spot the guy where you work who is the office pimp. He'll be able to introduce you to a madam. Be prepared to give the madam half of what you earn. Actually, she'll take her half and hand you yours. Be sure you have a telephone and an answering service. Your madam won't like it if she tries to reach you to tell you about a booking and can't. Later, after you've worked for the madam for a while, you'll be able to start your own book. That is, you can set up shop on your own based on the men you've met through the madam.

2. Explaining yourself:

People will begin to wonder how a previously poor chick like you suddenly has money to burn. Carefully plan your explanation *before* you start flashing all that money you'll be earning. Following are some examples of stories you may use:

a. Your rich aunt died. When asked, "How come you never mentioned a rich aunt?" reply, "Oh, didn't I? I'm sure I told you about her at that New Year's party when you first turned on to hash!" Then switch the subject by saying, "By the way, I've got this dynamite smoke that I've been dying to turn you on to."

b. You won the Mexican National Lottery. Explain that

you shared the ticket with someone who wants it to remain a secret for tax purposes, and so do you, so please
don't talk about it with anyone.

c. You've got an extra job doing free-lance manuscript
typing for those famous authors, Jeffers and Levitan.
(We'll never tell!)

3. What to do about your boyfriend:

Of course, he'll be curious about certain things, such as,
where you were last night, how come you've gotten yourself an answering service, where'd you get the money for
the new coat, is there another guy, where'd you learn to
do all those things he's wanted you to do in bed but which
you peristently refused, and why you are going on a weekend to the Bahamas and with whom. These may seem
very difficult matters to explain, but you don't have to
explain them. When these questions arise, simply blow in
your boy friend's ear and whisper in your sexiest voice,
"Let's go to bed and I'll tell you all about it." In bed, he'll
forget he ever asked.

4. Limiting yourself:

Decide for yourself what you will and will not do sexually
for money. Remember, the more you do, the more money
you'll earn. This means of earning money depends largely
on repeat business. Repeaters are the ones who got their
money's worth the first time.

5. Helpful hints to make you a better call girl:

a. Go to see some pornographic films. Take notes.

b. Ask the men you know what turns them on the most.

c. Open a savings account.

d. Get a good stock and investment adviser. (Offer him
yourself as his commission and put all your cash into your
stocks.)

e. Take some acting lessons.

f. Read the current bestsellers.

g. Subscribe to the *New York Times*, the *Wall Street
Journal*, *Time*, *Newsweek*, and *Screw* magazine.

h. Read Dr. Reuben's book.

i. Read Masters and Johnson.

j. Read Henry Miller.

k. Browse through your local pornography store for books on sex technique.

l. Learn the other words for: fellatio, cunnilingus, sexual intercourse. Ask the girl at the next desk.

m. Forget about joining Women's Lib.

n. Always carry pencil and small note pad for jotting down your number.

o. Learn how to spot cops. (Some clues: They wear white socks, their jackets bulge under their left arms, they have short hair, you can't reach them in the morning because they are in court testifying against the hookers they busted the night before.)

6. Free-lancing:

Once you have established your own "book" after having worked for a madam for a while, you may rightly want to set up your own operation. Try it. You may become a madam yourself someday. But initially, you will have to get some things together to be successful as an independent entrepreneur. Some basics:

a. Your own apartment with separate bedroom.

b. An alias under which to lease the apartment and have a phone installed.

c. A man who can act as a protector or collector of unpaid bills. (Not a pimp, just a friendly guy who likes you and would rough someone up for you.)

d. Establish a small bank account into which you put a portion of your money for payoffs to: your doorman, the cops, your muscle man, etc.

e. An open-dated airline ticket one-way to another city for fast getaways.

f. A tape recorder.

g. A Polaroid camera.

h. Large supply of towels.

i. Mirrors (full-length).

j. If you are really able to invest in hardware, a home video-tape recorder for instant pornographic pictures.

k. Address and phone number of an abortionist.

l. Address and phone number of a doctor who treats VD without reporting to the health department.

m. A contract with a book publisher for your memoirs.

Amateur Standing

1. Basic decisions:

a. Goals. Is this for fun or profit? Can you get a better job by putting out? Decide whether you are going to use your body to advance your career or simply to make yourself a happier person sexually.

b. Partners. These depend entirely on your goals. If you are seeking job advancement, social status, or friendly gifts of money, etc., then choose from this list: your boss, your boss's boss, the president of the company, the chairman of the board, the president of the union, the president of the United States, Chou En-Lai, Kosygin, an astronaut, Howard Hughes, a Greek shipping magnate, a famous author. If you are seeking nothing more than fun, select from this list: the New York Jets, the Eyewitness News Team, the U.S. Olympic Ski Team, the U.S. Military Academy at West Point, the Rolling Stones, Norman Mailer, Gore Vidal (don't invite them to the same party), any Democrat running for president (except George Wallace, Sam Yorty, and Wilbur Mills), Dick Cavett, Johnny Carson, Merv Griffin, David Frost, and David Susskind or anyone posing as them, Dick Levitan, H. Paul Jeffers.

2. Explaining yourself:

No need to.

3. What to do about your boy friend:

He'll take care of the matter himself.

4. Ways to have fun with a man:

   a. Tell him you're pregnant and want to have the baby.

   b. Invite his best friend to join you in bed but don't tell either of them in advance.

   c. Fellate him in a car, elevator, airplane, motorboat, or his office.

   d. Suggest you sit in the last row of the balcony and have intercourse when they're showing the coming attractions.

   e. Ask if that wasn't his wife you saw in the car across the street just as he was ringing your doorbell.

   f. Take a shower with him and scrub his back.

   g. Buy him a recording of the *1812 Overture* and tell him to hold back his orgasm until the cannons go off.

   h. Dress up like the genie in "I Dream of Jeanie."

   i. Buy him dinner once.

   j. Serve him a champagne cocktail in bed.

   k. Put a strawberry in the champagne glass.

   l. Put one in your navel.

   m. Put one anywhere else it will fit.

   n. Admire his sexual equipment.

   o. Make a plaster cast of his penis.

   p. Ask him to autograph it.

Appendix III.
Confessions
of a Call Girl

AUTHORS: How did you get started?

PLATINUM: I was working. I had a legitimate job. I was sweating bullets for nothing in a factory job. I was making $125 a week. I was putting in anywhere from eight to twelve hours a day. I figured there must be an easier way. One of my girls friends that I worked with told me that she did hooking on the side, so I went into hooking on the side.

AUTHORS: Before you did that you had to give it some thought.

PLATINUM: Well, you know, when I was a teenager, like from the age of fourteen, I was messing around, screwing, blowing, whatever. I was pretty experienced at seventeen. I lost my virginity, I forgot what a virgin is. Already at that stage it was old hat.

AUTHORS: What about the morality of it?
PLATINUM: The morality was out of it already. It was just a thought of doing it for free and then changing over to doing it for money, would that affect my life at all? It didn't because I wouldn't let it.
AUTHORS: When you first started, and you talked to your girl friend . . .
PLATINUM: I kept complaining to her about how much money I needed. Money goes through my hands like water. She was saying that in order to keep her bills up, and she had two kids, she was hooking on the side.
AUTHORS: So how did you start out?
PLATINUM: She fixed me up with a few of her people that she saw. They turned out to be nice people. I was not only having fun, I was making money, too.
AUTHORS: Then what happened?
PLATINUM: I met my former husband, and he took me out of the small town and brought me to New York. Because we figured it would be better for me to quit working and to do it at a larger scale. Hell, the money was good then.
AUTHORS: So your husband became your . . .
PLATINUM: No, he wasn't pimping. He said to me, if you're going to hook, hook for big money. He just showed me the larger scale. I was going for like ten dollars a throw, and when I came here it was forty, fifty, or a hundred dollars a throw.
AUTHORS: Is it like that now?
PLATINUM: You could clear two, three hundred dollars a night out there and no cuts, no nothing. The only risk was going to jail. The money isn't that good now.
AUTHORS: Where did you operate?
PLATINUM: The normal procedure was to go and get a hotel room. In midtown Manhattan, where all the tourists are. I worked Seventh Avenue. That's where all the big hotels are. I worked out of there until they found out what

I was doing and they politely asked me to leave.

AUTHORS: Did those guys at the hotels, the security men, ever ask for a payoff?

PLATINUM: No, I have never been hit for a payoff.

AUTHORS: Have you ever worked for anyone who had to pay off?

PLATINUM: No.

AUTHORS: Did you ever get caught by the police?

PLATINUM: Several times.

AUTHORS: What happened?

PLATINUM: They take you down, arrest you, book you. You sleep at a precinct overnight, then go to court. I have three arrests on the street. That's the trick, to tell who's a cop and who isn't. If you saw the policemen that arrested me, you would never, never say that they were policemen. They looked like goofy out-of-town businessmen. I swear to God they're actors. They're worse than the hookers.

AUTHORS: Give us an example of one of your arrests.

PLATINUM: I came out of the hotel one night. There were two guys out front. One was short with a big nose and wore glasses and was looking up at the buildings, and I said to myself that this can't be a cop. So I stood there a few minutes, and he approached me. Now he started the conversation, and I picked it up from there. He was dressed from out of town. I even looked at his socks. If he had white socks, he was a cop, or regulation socks, he was a cop. This guy had silk socks. He walked me around the corner and down the block. He said, "Let me hold your hand." He took my hand and put handcuffs on me. This is only a precaution for them.

AUTHORS: How long did you serve on that bust?

PLATINUM: I didn't do any time because everything got confused. I cried that I was from out of town when I was in front of the judge. There was nobody to say any different. The case was dismissed. That was my second bust. I was busted twice in one week and went before the same judge. But my second arrest came up first, so it got all confused. The judge dismissed the second one, too.

AUTHORS: What about your third arrest?

PLATINUM: I did fifteen days. Fifteen days is nothing. The first time you do it, it's a weird feeling. It's a big adjustment to make.

AUTHORS: You gave up the street, what led to that?

PLATINUM: My husband and I broke up. I went on welfare and tried to go to school and get a start on a straight life. I went along for three months, but I just couldn't take it no more and started hooking again. Through a girl friend I went to work in a house. You build your own book and then start to work for yourself.

AUTHORS: What's the most business you ever did in one day?

PLATINUM: I was working in a house and I saw forty guys in one day.

AUTHORS: Forty guys in one day?

PLATINUM: I came out of there with two hundred dollars.

AUTHORS: What time do you start in the morning?

PLATINUM: I used to start at eleven o'clock in the morning and come out of there at twelve o'clock at night. For a whole year I did this.

AUTHORS: You must have had callouses.

PLATINUM: You can't wear it out. (Laughter) It can go on indefinitely. Let me tell you, they nearly had to carry me out. But after a good night's sleep and a good hot douche, you're all set again.

AUTHORS: What's the difference between you and the street girls?

PLATINUM: If you get a street girl and put her next to me, you'd see the difference when we start talking. I still tend to talk slightly like a street girl because I was out there a long time. They curse constantly. I'm off the street now, and I don't have to talk tough. I try to talk like a lady. As you get into the higher-priced girls and into good houses you get girls that are more dignified, more sophisticated. I wouldn't go back to the streets. The girls are starving because of the current crackdown. It all depends on how discreet you are, of course. If you are going to act like a hooker, you won't last a week. Once you get picked up by the cops, you're known, and once you're known, it's all over but the teardrops.

AUTHORS: What are some examples of street talk?

PLATINUM: Trap, the nightly amount of money taken in. Jive bitch or funky bitch, a girl who's not doing anything, just fucking around out there. A hooker that held back money is a jive bitch. Track, the street or area you are working.

AUTHORS: Is there any special house talk?

PLATINUM: No, because you're not trying to impress anyone. A man is there, and you don't have to pick him up. You don't have to be a smartass. You have to be smart, be aware, be able to pick up on what a guy is there for. Anything that's done behind closed doors is okay. Out on the street, there's a law against it.

AUTHORS: What about a girl who is considering being a prostitute?

PLATINUM: I wouldn't recommend it. You have to be tough. I don't mean hard, tough. You have to have a constitution that will take the pressure. Everyone thinks being a prostitute is glamorous. Let me tell you. But it's not. You meet a lot of nice people, but of course you meet a lot of crazy people. There are a lot of perverts who come in under the pretense of seeing a girl normally and end up beating her or doing something violent and sadistic. Thank God there are places for them. The S and M places take the pressure off the plain old whorehouse where you come in, get your satisfaction, and you leave without any kind of hassle.

AUTHORS: You said you never made a payoff?

PLATINUM: I was shaken down once. A badge was flashed at me on the street, and I expected to be asked for money, but they wanted sex. So I paid them off in sex. It was better than going to jail. That happened twice. One of them became a regular of mine, and we got to be good friends.

AUTHORS: You're wearing a cross around your neck.

PLATINUM: I was raised a Roman Catholic. I believe in God. But I don't believe in everything that the church preaches. God loves prostitutes just as He loves everyone else. I think I'm doing humanity a great justice. Maybe I'm saving a little girl from being raped. It's not really a dirty business.

AUTHORS: Would you get out of the business? What would it take?

PLATINUM: I think just normal surroundings. I could be a bum or a millionaire.

AUTHORS: Are you happy?

PLATINUM: Yes. I have a lot of fun.

AUTHORS: How much do you make a week?

PLATINUM: A good week, three or four hundred dollars.

AUTHORS: That's good money.

PLATINUM: This business is not exactly the easiest job in the world. You have to be an actress. You have to be a wife, a mother, a daughter, and God knows what else. You have to generate a warm feeling for these guys. They say a hooker isn't supposed to have any kind of sexual feeling, but that's a lot of baloney. I'm a human being, I'm a woman, and if a guy stimulates me, I'm just like anybody else.

AUTHORS: Does your mother know the kind of work you do?

PLATINUM: At first she didn't know, but after several arrests I guess she put things together.

AUTHORS: Friends?

PLATINUM: I have friends that are friends, on the right side of the law.

AUTHORS: If you had the opportunity to tell the whole country something about prostitution, what would you say?

PLATINUM: Don't condemn a prostitute. She is doing you a favor. First of all, a married man that fools around is better off coming to a house with no strings attached. He pays his money and leaves. There's no love affair, no breaking up of a home. Second, I feel that prostitutes are doing humanity a favor, like I said. A lot of girls are saved from being raped. I think prostitution should be legalized.

About the Authors

Before merging their talents to become a book-writing team, H. PAUL JEFFERS and DICK LEVITAN worked separately as broadcast newsmen in New England and New York. While working together as an editor-reporter team for an all-news radio station, they decided to collaborate on a book exposing brutalities in the training of recruits in the United States Marine Corps. That book, *See Parris and Die*, met with an icy silence from the Marines, although some of the suggestions made by Jeffers and Levitan were quietly adopted by the Corps. *Sex in the Executive Suite* is their second collaboration.

H. Paul Jeffers is the author of nine books, an award-winning news writer and producer, a Fulbright scholar, and an educator. Dick Levitan's unflinching investigative reporting has won him numerous awards in New England, New York, and New Jersey. He is a guest lecturer in broadcast journalism and investigative reporting at several universities and colleges. Jeffers and Levitan are at work on a third book together, and each is also at work on a book of his own.